P9-APD-393

North Woods Journal

A MINNESOTA NATURE CALENDAR

Stone Ridge Press
2515 Garthus Road
Wrenshall, MN 55797
www.stoneridgepress.com
sparkystensaas@hotmail.com
TO ORDER: 1.800.678.7006

North Woods Journal

© 2005 by Mark Sparky Stensaas & Ryan Marshik. All rights reserved.
Except for short excerpts for review purposes, no part of this book may
be reproduced or transmitted in any form by any means, electronic or
mechanical, including photocopying, without permission in writing
from the publisher.

Printed in Canada by Friesens
10 9 8 7 6 5 4 3 2 1 First Edition

Graphic Designer: Mark Sparky Stensaas

ISBN 0-9760313-0-2

Acknowledgements

No book is an island unto itself. We'd like to thank Joy Dey for her input on design and layout. Catherine Long
helped keep the text concise and clear. Thanks also to our proofreaders who caught all those little mistakes
that eluded the author's eyes. Naturalist extraordinaire, Larry Weber, proofread the phenology text to make
sure that all our facts and dates jived. Special thanks to Bridget Banks and Shari Marshik.

Mark Sparky Stensaas & Ryan Marshik
October 2004

North Woods Journal

A MINNESOTA NATURE CALENDAR

written by *Mark Sparky Stensaas*
photographs by *Ryan Marshik & Mark Sparky Stensaas*

Stone Ridge Press

Dedicated to all
who have a passion for
the North Woods

What is the *North Woods Journal* ?

North Woods Journal is a week-by-week phenology guide to northern Minnesota—a calendar of what's happening outside each week. It's a notebook for you to write nature observations throughout the year—your own personal phenology treasury. "But wait. What the heck is phenology?" you may be asking. It is NOT the study of the caustic poisonous crystalline acidic compound called phenol. Nor is it the pseudoscience popular in the 1800s of predicting the character and intelligence of a person based on their skull shape—that is actually "phrenology." So, I suppose, an explanation is in order. *Webster's New Collegiate Dictionary* defines phenology as a "branch of science dealing with the relations between climate and periodic biological phenomena [such] as bird migration or plant flowering." Simply put, it is the study of nature's yearly events. If you note when the hummingbirds return to your sugar-water feeder each May or the date the Sugar Maple in your front yard peaks each fall, then you already are a phenologist.

Phenology phor Phun

But what good is phenology? The most basic answer may be that it is fun. There is incredible satisfaction in observing a natural event, recording it and then reliving that experience for years to come. A glance at a page of notes and sketches from a hike with a friend will bring back a stream of memories. Gathering your phenology finds is a great excuse for getting out on a canoe trip, hiking at a nearby nature center or even strolling around the back yard.

A phenology journal is also a cure for short-term memory loss. Have you ever said, "Boy, the robins sure came back late this year."? A glance back through your nature notes in your copy of *North Woods Journal* would quickly show if the robins were indeed tardy, or if other late dates had been forgotten.

But phenology can also be a soothsayer of coming calamity and, therefore, a call to action. One good example of phenologic information playing an important role in conservation is the Breeding Bird Survey of the United States Geologic Survey. This yearly event is run on hundreds of routes all over North America and is conducted by amateur birders, not federal scientists. The surveys of birds are all completed in June and each of the 50 stops on a route are the same from year to year. Decades of data have been analyzed and the results showed both good and bad trends. Increases in Merlins were encouraging but a sharp decline in the population of Kirtland's Warblers in Michigan was alarming. Studies made a direct link to one culprit: the Brown-headed Cowbird. Female cowbirds lay their eggs in the nests of other birds, including Kirtland's Warblers. The fast-growing cowbird chicks outcompete the young warblers for food or shove them right out of the nest. Cowbird control has now allowed the Kirtland's Warbler population to rebound. Phenology in action!

Cavemen to Thoreau: Historic Phenology

Keeping track of nature's seasonal happenings is nothing new. Discovery of Chauvet Cave in 1994 revealed that over 35,000 years ago, peoples in southern France recorded the animals found in their valley.

Painstakingly they painted their observations of Ice Age bison and horses onto the walls and ceilings of their cave. The accurate and expressive figures most likely played a role in shamanistic hunting rights.

In the North Woods, red pictographs created hundreds of years ago with a mixture of vermilion and sturgeon oil can still be found on some rock faces in the canoe country along the Canadian border. Carl Gawboy, professor of American Indian Studies at the College of St. Scholastica, believes these drawings of Moose and "water panthers" and hands and people were actually representations of the stars. Early hunters, he conjectures, would need to know when it was time to return home in the spring and the stars were their seasonal guides. Carl notes that if these pictographs were simply ancient graffiti, we'd find them all over, but we don't.

Written over 2000 years ago, the Bible contains some of the earliest known nature notes. Proverbs imparts weather knowledge, "The north wind brings forth rain; and a backbiting tongue, angry looks." (Proverbs 25: 23) and also some ornithological observations, "Like a sparrow in its flitting, like a swallow in its flying, a curse that is causeless does not alight." (Proverbs 26: 2). King Solomon later reveals a true appreciation of the natural world, "Four things on earth are small, but they are exceedingly wise: the ants are a people not strong, yet they provide their food in the summer; the badgers are a people not mighty, yet they make their homes in the rocks; the locusts have no king, yet all of them march in rank; the lizard you can take in your hands, yet it is in kings' palaces." (Proverbs 30: 24-28). He also expresses true admiration for wild things, "Three things are too wonderful for me; four I do not understand: the way of an eagle in the sky, the way of a serpent on a rock, the way of a ship on the high seas, and the way of a man with a maiden." (Proverbs 30: 18-19).

Pliny the Elder (A.D. 23 to A.D. 79) was not only a Roman senator and naval commander but a great observer of his fellow man and the natural world. In his volumes of *Natural History*, He makes some very astute observations, "Dogs keep running when they drink at the Nile, for fear of becoming a prey to the voracity of the crocodile.", some interesting observations, "Bears when first born are shapeless masses of white flesh a little larger than mice, their claws alone being prominent…The mother then licks them gradually into proper shape." and some downright wrong observations, "All men possess in their bodies a poison which acts upon serpents; and the human saliva it is said, makes them take to flight, as though they had been touched with boiling water. The same substance it is said, destroys them the moment it enters their throat." Pliny the Elder died in a valiant attempt to rescue the citizens of Pompeii by ship during the Mount Vesuvius eruption.

Undoubtedly the most famous phenologist was the early naturalist-writer Henry David Thoreau (1817-1862). His many volumes of nature journals (published as *Journals* in 1906) are filled with the dates of blooming flowers, ripening fruit and migrant bird arrivals—and even a few truly awful sketches. I once compared his spring dates for birds returning to the Concord, Massachusetts area (42 degrees North latitude) with the dates of the same species returning to the Twin Cities of Minnesota (45 degrees North latitude). Though separated by 1200 miles and 150 years many of the arrival dates were very close. Nature can stay quite consistent at similar latitudes in similar ecosystems despite the upheaval and changes created by man.

Thoreau's Transcendentalist view of Nature inspired him to explore and experience the natural world, taking from it life lessons and material for his philosophical essays. But Henry David was conflicted when it came to his cold analyzation of plant specimens, scientific naming and elaborate charts; these were not

Transcendentalist ways. On Christmas day 1851, Thoreau lamented, "What sort of science is that which enriches the understanding but robs the imagination?" and later, "I have become sadly scientific." Nonetheless, he continued in his obsessive notetaking, scientific collections and identifications.

Thoreau the phenologist was revealed early on when as a recent Harvard graduate and rookie teacher, he proclaimed to his pupils that he could tell the month by what was blooming in the nearby woods. And after 15 more years of botanizing, I'm sure he could pinpoint the exact week by the plants in flower. His zeal for blooming, fruiting, sprouting and shedding dates never abated. "It will take you half a lifetime to find out where to look for the earliest flower." He wrote on April 2, 1856. Late in his short life, he took a decade of phenology dates and combined them into detailed monthly charts illustrating a typical phenological year for Concord, Massachusetts—the exact goal of the *North Woods Journal* for northern Minnesota.

Inspiration

Jim Gilbert was the first phenologist I had ever met. I helped Jim band birds at Carver Park in 1980 while still in high school, though my main memory of that day was being bit by a Rose-breasted Grosbeak whose thick beak easily drew blood. His folksy 1983 book, *Jim Gilbert's Nature Notebook*, laid out month by month the natural happenings around the Minnesota Landscape Arboretum southwest of the Twin Cities. In the book Jim listed years of dates for such quirky natural events as "first meal of sweet corn out of the garden" and "Canada Thistle beginning to shed seeds on parachutes" and "first turtles out sunning." These little charts inspired me to keep my own phenology records.

I started filling little spiral notebooks with bird observations. But I could never find them a year or two later to compare dates of events. Switching to the hardcover 8 1/2 x 11-inch artist's sketchbooks enabled me to fit three to five years of notes and sketches before having to buy a new one. But I always felt that the blank books were a bit too stark and uninviting. A journal book with seasonal photos, nature notes and room to write and sketch would be just the ticket.

The motivation to finally start this project resulted from a friendship with fellow photographer, Ryan Marshik. Ryan and I worked together at an outdoor gear shop in Duluth where we discovered a shared energy for the North Woods and recording that beauty on film (and now in pixels). Our photo travels have taken us to the U.P. of Michigan, White Sands National Park in New Mexico, Saguaro National Park in southeast Arizona, Utah's Bryce Canyon, Zion and Grand Staircase-Escalante National Parks and most recently, Yellowstone. But home for both of us is northern Minnesota. Out of our many trips to the North Shore and Boundary Waters Canoe Area Wilderness, and our passion for photography and phenology, comes the *North Woods Journal*.

North Woods Journal is the result of these inspirations and collaborations. It is not only designed to get you started in taking seasonal nature notes—the building blocks to a phenological understanding of the North Woods—but also to inspire, with beautiful photographs and fascinating facts about our local flora and fauna.

Layout and Design

The journal is arranged on a calendar year with each month divided into five 6-day periods. We chose not to list days of the week as this would limit the journal's use to a single year. Besides, days of the week are moot when it comes to natural events. On the right hand side of the spread is a side bar called *What's happenin'* that highlights the phenologic events that typically occur during that week each year. These dates are based on my 25 years of field notes from the North Woods. Of course, they are average dates and they may vary from year to year and from place to place. Your stomping grounds could be a week or more ahead or behind these dates. Weather also influences the timing of bird migration, bloom dates and insect hatches.

Photo Credits and information on ordering prints are found just before the *Index*. On the same spread is a *Sunrise/Sunset Table* and a ten-year *Full Moon Chart*, both useful tools in planning a hike or photo trip. Use the *Index* to find more information on species of flora or fauna encountered during the year.

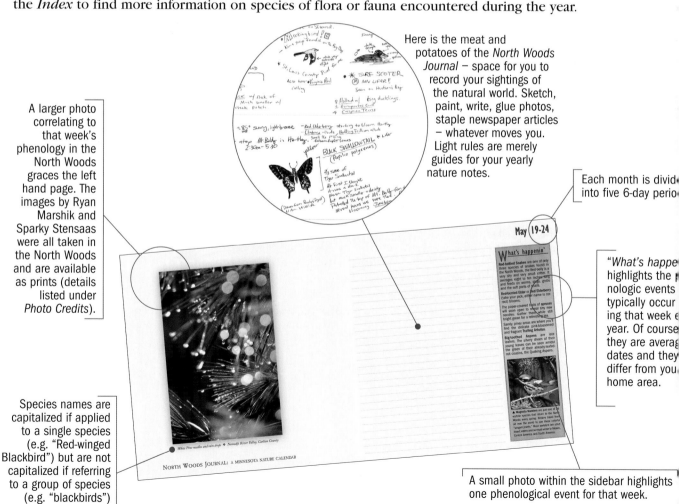

Here is the meat and potatoes of the *North Woods Journal* — space for you to record your sightings of the natural world. Sketch, paint, write, glue photos, staple newspaper articles — whatever moves you. Light rules are merely guides for your yearly nature notes.

A larger photo correlating to that week's phenology in the North Woods graces the left hand page. The images by Ryan Marshik and Sparky Stensaas were all taken in the North Woods and are available as prints (details listed under *Photo Credits*).

Each month is divided into five 6-day periods

"*What's happenin'* highlights the phenologic events that typically occur during that week each year. Of course, they are average dates and they differ from your home area.

Species names are capitalized if applied to a single species (e.g. "Red-winged Blackbird") but are not capitalized if referring to a group of species (e.g. "blackbirds")

A small photo within the sidebar highlights one phenological event for that week.

May 19-24

What's happenin'

NORTH WOODS JOURNAL: A MINNESOTA NATURE CALENDAR

How to Use and Abuse your *North Woods Journal*

Five years from now we hope this book is a real mess. We want coffee stains on the cover, ink smears and eraser tears in the paper and old mosquito carcasses smushed between the pages. *North Woods Journal* is not only designed to write your weekly nature observations but also to glue photos in, sketch your discoveries, press flowers and feathers and staple relevant newspaper articles. This is your Minnesota nature notebook; go ahead and personalize it. If you are a neat freak that likes to keep your books in good shape then we recommend writing and drawing with pencil or felt tip pen to prevent bleed through of the ink on to the next page.

But most importantly, we want you to have years of weekly nature notes, drawings and photos that will bring you back to that week a year ago...or two years ago...or five years ago. And now when Uncle Joe boldly claims that it has never snowed this much in March before, you can prove him wrong. Fill it up and when you find yourself writing in microscopic script in the margins, go out and get another one. I guarantee you that the filled *North Woods Journals* will become more treasured the older they get. You will get great enjoyment out of rereading your journals for years to come.

Here are some ideas of Natural events to note each year:

- ❑ When the Tree Swallows return to the nest box
- ❑ The first snow that accumulates on the ground
- ❑ Blooming of the crocuses
- ❑ Ice-up of a nearby lake
- ❑ Ice-out of the same lake
- ❑ Birds at the feeder and what days they arrive and depart
- ❑ First ripe tomato in the garden
- ❑ Peak fall color on maples, birches, aspen and oak
- ❑ Ripe blueberries...strawberries...chokecherries
- ❑ Date when first bitten by a mosquito
- ❑ Last day snow patches dot your lawn
- ❑ Smells (First skunk...Balsam Poplar buds...Fall woodsmoke)
- ❑ First White-tailed Deer fawn

Your notes don't have to be natural happenings either. Human activity can be phenological:

- ❑ First child out flying a kite in spring
- ❑ First sunbather in spring (note the temperature and compare to a day of the same temperature in fall to see if you can find any sunbathers...I bet not!)
- ❑ Sound of the first droning lawn mower in the neighborhood
- ❑ First street sweepers out
- ❑ Date the outdoor Dairy Queen opens
- ❑ Date the outdoor Dairy Queen closes
- ❑ Farmers cutting hay for first time...second time...third time?
- ❑ First "back-to-school" ads on TV
- ❑ When you see the first Christmas lights
- ❑ First fool out on the lake ice in a truck

Jumbled ice shards on Lake Superior ❖ *Minnesota Point, Duluth*

NORTH WOODS JOURNAL: A MINNESOTA NATURE CALENDAR

What's happenin'

Cirrus clouds are the highest clouds, occurring five to six miles up in the sky. At this elevation temperatures are so cold that the moisture in the cloud is all in the form of ice crystals. Atmospheric winds often blow them into shapes we call "mares tails."

Windchills can be brutal this time of year. First quantified by a team of scientists in Antarctica before World War II, this relative temperature measures the effect of wind on how cold we feel. A minus 20 degree F windchill means that heat is being whisked away from our body at the same rate as on a minus 20 degree day with no wind.

Beneath the thick ice on the pond is a world of active **aquatic insects**: backswimmers, predaceous diving beetles, water boatmen, giant water bugs and dragonfly nymphs.

▲ Summering on the "Arctic Riviera" of Hudson Bay, **Snowy Owls** move south during winters of scarcity. A few end up in northern Minnesota. From fence posts, telephone poles and rooftops, Snowys scan for rabbits, pheasants, pigeons and rats. Winter hay fields also make a fine substitute for tundra.

Jack Pine & falling snow ❖ *St. Louis River Gorge, Thomson*

NORTH WOODS JOURNAL: A MINNESOTA NATURE CALENDAR

What's happenin'

"Fat" birds are just cold birds trying to stay warm. They are fluffing their feathers to trap more air for better insulation, essentially creating a "poofier" and thereby warmer down coat. Ornithologists call this survival technique, **piloerection**.

January thaws are a near annual event in the frozen Northland. Temperatures may soar to above freezing for a day or two and then plummet back down to our normal midwinter deep freeze.

Appearing at sunflower seed feeders even before the sun comes up are the mighty mites of the bird world – **Black-capped Chickadees**. Maintaining an internal temperature of 104 degrees Fahrenheit on frigid January days is no easy feat for a tiny ball of fluff, which must spend 20 times longer feeding now than it would on a warm spring day.

▲ **Evening Grosbeaks** (above) and Pine Grosbeaks may or may not show up at your feeders this winter. These large finches are irruptive species that move constantly in search of food. Away from the sunflower seed feeders they eat ash seeds, maple buds and birch buds.

Softstem Bulrushes and winter shadows ❖ *Seagull Lake, Boundary Waters Canoe Area Wilderness*

NORTH WOODS JOURNAL: A MINNESOTA NATURE CALENDAR

What's happenin'

Road-hunting **Common Ravens** fly up and down country highways looking for fresh road-killed squirrels, rabbits and the *crème de la crème* – White-tailed Deer. If a carcass is not opened, the ravens must wait for coyotes or wolves or dogs to tear through the hide.

The whiskey jack – better known as the **Gray Jay** – is quite suited for life in the North. In autumn they gather food, mash it, mix it with their saliva and stick the gooey pellets to branches and under bark. The saliva may even act as a food preservative. These tiny marble-sized caches will fuel the jays through lean winter months. And they will need the extra energy as Gray Jays actually start nesting in March when temperatures may sink below zero and there can be three feet of snow on the ground.

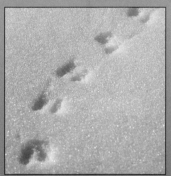

▲ Deep snow may be the bane of some mammals, but it is a boon to mice and voles that spend the winter beneath the white stuff. Air pockets between the ice crystals insulate from the cold. It may be 20 degrees below zero F at snow level but 30 degrees ABOVE zero under two feet of fluffy snow.

Wave-splashed boulders on Lake Superior ❖ *Tettegouche State Park*

NORTH WOODS JOURNAL: A MINNESOTA NATURE CALENDAR

What's happenin'

Red Squirrels dig apparently random holes in the snow looking for cones stashed last fall. Amazingly, their recovery rate is over 90 percent. Forgotten seeds may germinate into tomorrow's trees.

Beaver are snug and warm in their lodges. Cached branches under the ice are the foodstuffs of their winter pantry. Lips that close behind their big front teeth allow them to swim out, chomp onto a branch and swim back without ingesting water and drowning.

Wave-shaped **snow patterns** form on area lakes. The designs are the product of strong winds.

Check your **Mountain Ash trees** for fruit-eating visitors from the West. Rocky Mountain residents, the **Varied Thrush** and **Townsend's Solitaire**, occasionally show up in the winter.

▲ **Sundogs**, or **parhelia**, are the small partial rainbows flanking the sun on very cold days. They are caused by sunlight passing through ice crystals and refracting in the upper atmosphere. This phenomenon is most common in December and January but can be seen nearly any month.

White-breasted Nuthatch feeding its way down an aspen trunk ❖ *Duluth*

North Woods Journal: A Minnesota Nature Calendar

What's happenin'

Most bull **Moose** have dropped their antlers by now; only a few still retain them. Once shed, the antlers are quickly chewed into oblivion by calcium-craving rodents. Not only do the rodents ingest precious minerals, but also their forever-growing rodent teeth are kept in check by the gnawing. **Deer Mice**, White-footed Mice, **Red Squirrels** and **Porcupines** are the usual suspects.

A booming call echoes through the silent forest, "WHO COOKS FOR YOU...WHO COOKS FOR YOU ALLLLL!" On calm nights in deciduous woods you may hear the distinctive hoots of a **Barred Owl**. Try imitating the sound. Wait a few minutes and try again. You may be treated to a close encounter of the owl kind.

Inside the ball-shaped **gall** on goldenrod is the grub of a **Gall Fly** that laid its egg in the stem last summer.

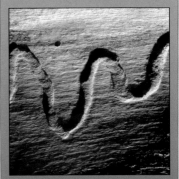

▲ Hiding under the bark of dead and dying trees are some amazing etchings. These boring patterns are created by rarely seen **bark beetles**. Each species makes a distinctive pattern as the adults burrow under the bark, lay their eggs and the larvae gnaw tunnels out and away from the egg chamber.

Winter sunset viewed through ice shard ❖ *Minnesota Point, Duluth*

NORTH WOODS JOURNAL: A MINNESOTA NATURE CALENDAR

What's happenin'

Red Squirrels camp out at feeders with black oil sunflower seeds. Their normal territories are only about 100 to 200 yards in diameter so several squirrels may move in to make your feeder home. But there is no truce here, and brief but fierce battles are common events.

A few hardy ducks will spend the winter in the North if there is available open water. **Common Goldeneyes** prefer the pools below rapids of larger rivers where they dive for aquatic insects, fish and crayfish. Some may also be found on Lake Superior. Other species that overwinter on the "Big Lake" include **Mallards** and **Common Mergansers**. But how can ducks stand the cold water on exposed legs? Arterial blood is actually pre-cooled by its proximity to cold venous blood returning to the heart.

▲ This is an unusual rufous, or red morph, **Ruffed Grouse**. Most we see are gray (see photo December 7-12). In Minnesota, reds are more common in the south. Ruffed Grouse are named for their neck feathers that can be erected into a kind of collar or "ruff."

Gray Jay looking for a handout ❖ *Knife Lake, Boundary Waters Canoe Area Wilderness*

NORTH WOODS JOURNAL: A MINNESOTA NATURE CALENDAR

What's happenin'

Snow shapes the landscape. **Black Spruce, White Spruce and Balsam Fir** all share a similar conical shape. The downswept branches shed snow as efficiently as an A-frame cabin. This saves the branches from breaking under heavy snow loads and helps them to survive further north than pines.

Eastern Cottontails feed on shrub stems in the evening. You can tell a rabbit-nipped stem from a deer-stripped stem by how neatly it is clipped off. Since deer have no upper teeth, the branch is stripped; cottontails neatly clip the stem.

Every 8 to 11 years **Snowshoe Hare** populations crash. Recent evidence suggests that overbrowsing during peak years causes willows to produce more young shoots which are laced with phenolic glycosides – a very effective hare repellant. Less food equals less reproduction.

▲ A sighting of a **Boreal Owl** is a real treat. It is one North America's rarest owls. Unfortunately, hunting during daylight hours often means that the Boreal is starving. Crusty, deep snow and low populations of mice and voles all make finding food in winter a difficult proposition.

Shore ice at sunrise ❖ *Palisade Head, Lake Superior*

NORTH WOODS JOURNAL: A MINNESOTA NATURE CALENDAR

What's happenin'

Mating season has begun for **Northern Flying Squirrels**, **Gray Squirrels** and **Red Squirrels**. Chasing and wrestling are just part of squirrel courtship.

Yellow patches on the trunks of White Pines are where feeding **Porcupines** have gnawed through to the pine's inner bark. They seem to prefer White Pine, Sugar Maple and White Spruce.

Large weasels called **Fishers** are a very effective predator of Porkies. They attack the face and try to flip the spiny snack on its back to get at the soft underbelly. I once followed a Fisher that seemed to be searching for Porkies only in pines that had been recently gnawed. **Bobcats** are also fairly efficient predators of Porcupines.

Leaflike **swirls of frost** form on window panes in extremely cold weather.

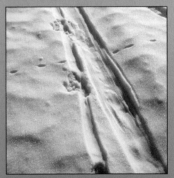

▲ **River Otters**, though rarely seen, can be easily tracked along winter watercourses. Their low-slung body leaves a shallow trench interspersed by long slides. Hillsides, riverbanks, lakeshore bluffs and even Beaver lodges are favorite sliding hills for the playful otter.

Great Gray Owl hunting voles and mice ❖ *Sax–Zim Bog, St. Louis County*

NORTH WOODS JOURNAL: A MINNESOTA NATURE CALENDAR

What's happenin'

Red-osier Dogwood lives up to its name in winter. Pigments in the bark increase when sunlight is able to reach the branches. The red stems stand out against the backdrop of snow (see photo November 19-24). Some willow shrub branches are now turning bright yellow.

The mournful hooting of **Great Horned Owls** signals another mating season has arrived. They are the first bird in Minnesota to nest and will often be on eggs by early March. Why so early? The eggs need nearly a month of incubation, followed by a month and a half of nest time for the young and another month is required before they can fly. That is a long adolescence in the bird world. In winter Great Horneds subsist on squirrels and rabbits but supplement with early-emerging skunks, domestic cats and even other owls.

▲ Gliding into your bird feeder under the cover of darkness is the big-eyed and very nocturnal **Northern Flying Squirrel**. Loose flaps of skin between their front and hind legs allow them to launch off a tree trunk and glide 30 feet or more. Daylight hours are spent snoozing in old woodpecker holes.

King of the woodpeckers: A male Pileated Woodpecker ❖ *near Shagawa Lake, Ely*

NORTH WOODS JOURNAL: A MINNESOTA NATURE CALENDAR

What's happenin'

A familiar odor returns to the Northland: "*eau de skunk*." Though **Striped Skunks** do not hibernate, they are dormant most of the winter, only appearing when temperatures become mild.

Timber Wolf pack dynamics are very interesting this time of year. February is mating season and howling frequency increases. Step outside on a quiet night in wolf country and give a listen. Minnesota is now home to over 3000 wolves, the most in the lower forty-eight states. Their range is even edging near the Twin Cities.

Listen late at night for the high-pitched monotone "tooting" of the diminutive **Saw-whet Owl**; a bird no bigger than a family-size can of beans. They nest in old Northern Flicker and Pileated Woodpecker holes in overmature aspens.

▲ This is the work of the **Pileated Woodpecker**; a huge prehistoric-looking bird that dines on big **Black Carpenter Ants** found deep inside rotting trees. Jackhammerlike blows gets access to the ants' burrows. It then flicks its long, barbed tongue down the hole to hook ants.

White-tailed Deer does ❖ *Jay Cooke State Park, Carlton County*

NORTH WOODS JOURNAL: A MINNESOTA NATURE CALENDAR

What's happenin'

Your feeder can be a very active place after dark. **Red-backed Voles** emerge from their snow tunnels to feed on fallen seeds, and in turn, **Barred Owls** or **Saw-whet Owls** come in to feed on unwary voles. **Northern Flying Squirrels** glide in for a midnight snack of sunflower seeds. **White-tailed Deer** and **Raccoons** may also make a visit.

Now that the weather is a bit milder, **Red Squirrels** seem to be more active, constantly at the feeders from dawn to dusk. I timed one little guy who was devouring sunflower seeds at a rate of six to eight per minute, which included time spent picking up and rejecting bad seeds.

Carefully check the snow's surface on a thawing day and you will be surprised at the number of **insects** and **spiders** that are out and about.

▲ The masked bandit of the bird world may show up at your feeder this winter. **Northern Shrikes** are barely robin-sized, but they are efficient predators of mice, frogs and small birds – even your cute little feeder birds. Enjoy the shrike's presence as part of the circle of life.

"Pancake ice" rounded by jostling in wave swells ❖ *Minnesota Point, Duluth*

North Woods Journal: A Minnesota Nature Calendar

What's happenin'

Common Ravens are building new stick nests or adding on to last year's effort. The male and female both participate. Also watch for their tandem acrobatic flights of twists, turns and barrel rolls – any stunt pilot would be jealous!

Red Foxes are now paired up and in mating mode. Females (vixens) dig dens in sandy hillsides. Litters average five pups and are born in May after a gestation period of 51 to 53 days. Their home range may be as small as 160 acres or as large as 1500 acres.

Our resident aliens, the **European Starlings**, are changing garb. Their black bills are becoming yellow as the mating season approaches.

March is the **snowiest month** in Minnesota. The heaviest snowfalls are usually on the ridges above the North Shore of Lake Superior.

▲ Humans are not the only mammals who gather maple sap. **Red Squirrels** gnaw on maple branches and then lap up the sweet treat. They will also pilfer oozing birch and maple sap from the rows of holes drilled by Yellow-bellied Sapsuckers, a common forest woodpecker.

Near albino Red-tailed Hawk ❖ *West of Alexandria, Douglas County*

NORTH WOODS JOURNAL: A MINNESOTA NATURE CALENDAR

What's happenin'

Keep your ears open for the liquid trills of the first male **Red-winged Blackbirds** staking out territories in cattail marshes. Females return several weeks later and pick a mate. The most desirable male is one with the best territory: And the best territory is often secured by males displaying the biggest red wing patches called epaulettes (see photo April 1-6). Studies have shown that the males with the largest epaulettes are best able to retain prime territories.

Melting snow reveals shrubs and small trees whose bark has been eaten off by **mice**, **Eastern Cottontail Rabbits** and **Snowshoe Hares**. Gnaw marks three feet above the ground are not the sign of a giant breed of rabbit but evidence of the high snow line from the previous winter.

▲ **Ring-billed Gulls** return to the Northland and, most famously, to Canal Park in Duluth. Remember, there is no such thing as a "seagull"; all gulls have a specific name. Nineteen species have been recorded in Minnesota, but only Ring-billed, Herring and Franklin's Gulls regularly breed.

Sunset reflection on a thawing Beaver River ❖ *St. Louis County*

NORTH WOODS JOURNAL: A MINNESOTA NATURE CALENDAR

What's happenin'

The sugar-rich sap of **Sugar Maples** flows freely on sunny warm spring days with below freezing nights. Maple syrup producers begin tapping trees. It takes 40 gallons of sap on average to make one gallon of syrup. Red Maples, Box Elder and Silver Maples can also be tapped.

The first mammalian hibernators wake up; **Eastern** and **Least Chipmunks** are seen in lingering snow below feeders or near woodpiles. Winter was spent in their snug nest of leaves in a burrow that may be 30 feet long and 3 feet below ground. Mating takes place soon after waking. Females will have a litter of four or five young in April after a 31-day gestation.

Porcupines will clamber up the bendy branches of pussy willows to feed on the male flowers (catkins).

▲ Fuzzy, silver **Pussy Willow** catkins will shed pollen in a few weeks. There are 15 species of willows in Minnesota but not a single species called Diamond Willow. The "diamonds," so popular with walking stick carvers, are wood that has grown around branches killed by a fungal disease.

Melting icicles in the splash zone ❖ *Stoney Point, North Shore*

NORTH WOODS JOURNAL: A MINNESOTA NATURE CALENDAR

What's happenin'

Bald Eagles move north in large numbers. Over 800 in a single day have been seen from western Skyline Drive in Duluth! Though a few eagles remain in the North feeding on road kills, most have been wintering along open stretches of the Mississippi River near locks and dams where stunned and dead fish make the living easy.

Crows are flying to and fro with grass and sticks in their beaks. This can only mean one thing – it's nest-building time. On rare occasions crows will breed communally: Yearling crows may help the mated pair raise their nestlings.

A hardy few **American Robins** will spend the winter in the North feeding on crabapples and Mountain-Ash berries, but their territorial song is not heard until late March or early April.

▲ Minnesota has several species of butterflies that hibernate as adults. Sunny, warm spring days awaken them, and they fly about feeding on oozing tree sap. Watch for Comptons Tortoiseshell, Milbert's Tortoiseshell, Eastern Comma and the **Mourning Cloak** (above) in late March or early April.

An early-returning male Red-winged Blackbird endures a spring snow squall

NORTH WOODS JOURNAL: A MINNESOTA NATURE CALENDAR

What's happenin'

Tundra Swans congregate on the St. Louis River estuary near Duluth. After wintering along the Atlantic Seaboard they return to their Arctic breeding grounds via northern Minnesota.

Woodchucks begin stretching their legs after a long sleep. Indeed most "whistle pigs" curled up in their burrow before the last hard frost of autumn. Their burrow is a crazy network of tunnel 25 to 40 feet long and four feet down.

Black Bears are "bearly" awake. Some emerge in late March while others in cooler spots wait until mid-April.

Roadside flashes of gray and white means the **Dark-eyed Juncos** are back. Can't see the dark eyes at 60 miles per hour? Look for the white outer tail feathers as the birds scatter off the road's shoulder.

▲ **Eastern Bluebirds** along with Red-winged Blackbirds (males first), Mourning Doves and Common Grackles are the first migrant songbirds to return. Bluebird boxes should be ready by late March. Put up a pair of nest boxes about 20 feet apart to minimize battles between bluebirds and Tree Swallows.

Columns of basalt splotched with Xanthoria lichens ❖ *Grand Marais Harbor*

North Woods Journal: A Minnesota Nature Calendar

What's happenin'

Eastern Garter Snakes begin emerging from their below ground hibernaculums on warm spring days.

What a **schizophrenic month**! One year it may be 80 degrees and we are out gardening in shorts. The next year, on the same day, we could be skiing in a howling snowstorm with below-zero wind chills. That's spring in the North Woods.

"Peeent...peent...peent." **American Woodcocks** give nasal calls from young aspen stands before launching into spectacular mating flights. They spiral upwards for several hundred feet – a delicate twittering comes from air rushing between stiff wing feathers – then a death-defying plummet to earth only to land inches from where they took off. It all takes place under the cover of "duskness" for the benefit of nearby females.

▲ Ponds, rivers and shallow lakes lose their ice first and are soon filled with ducks. This **Green-winged Teal** is in "nuptial" or prime breeding plumage. Showy males mate with the drab females, but once nest building is done, he splits, leaving the female to incubate the eggs alone.

Spot of Lake Superior sunrise light ❖ *Tettegouche State Park*

NORTH WOODS JOURNAL: A MINNESOTA NATURE CALENDAR

What's happenin'

Ice-out begins. A strong wind can clear a lake out in a few hours even though the ice may have measured several feet thick a week ago. The ice literally rots as water fills spaces in the disintegrating mass. The stronger spring sun has created a honeycombed mass of upright ice needles known as "chandelier ice" or "candle ice."

Get out the reading glasses. Miniscule scarlet flowers bloom on **Beaked Hazel** bushes.

Our **Eastern Phoebe** friends – the birds that build mud nests under the eaves of our cabins, sheds and saunas – have returned and are happily singing "FEE-BEE" from conspicuous perches.

Soon after the ice goes out, our Minnesota state bird, the **Common Loon**, returns. Listen for their haunting calls and mournful wails.

▲ One of the first woodland flowers to poke its head out of last year's dead leaves is the **Round-lobed Hepatica**. Snow patches may still linger, but hepatica perseveres. Petals are not really petals but actually sepals that can be bluish, pinkish or whitish.

Tenacious Northern White Cedar roots ❖ *Jay Cooke State Park, Carlton County*

NORTH WOODS JOURNAL: A MINNESOTA NATURE CALENDAR

What's happenin'

Flashes of iridescent blue and a gurgling bubbly song overhead signals that the **Tree Swallows** have returned.

"Thump, thump, thump, thrrrrrrrrrr." **Ruffed Grouse** begin drumming. Each deep thump is actually a tiny sonic boom – air rushing into the vacuum created by the flapping wings. A favorite drumming log may be used for decades, generations of the birds actually wearing a depression in the surface.

Male flowers (catkins) of **Quaking Aspen** are descended. **Speckled Alder** catkins are shedding pollen.

Like a henhouse full of chickens, **Wood Frogs** cackle from temporary pools. A cacophony of "peeps" is the mating frenzy of **Spring Peepers**. Also listen for the running-your-finger-down-a-comb call of the **Boreal Chorus Frog**.

▲ Dawn dancing is the preferred male display of **Sharp-tailed Grouse**. Traditional leks (dancing grounds) are used for decades. Females watch nearby as the males inflate their purple neck sacks, erect their orange eye combs then arc their wings and perform a foot-stamping dance.

Spring Beauty opening on one of the first warm days of spring ❖ *Jay Cooke State Park, Carlton County*

NORTH WOODS JOURNAL: A MINNESOTA NATURE CALENDAR

What's happenin'

Woodpeckers don't "sing" in the usual sense, but the male's drumming on resonant tree branches serves the same purpose. It says to other males, "Hey, this is my territory so stay out." And to females it signals, "C'mon over, I'm ready to mate." Clever **Yellow-bellied Sapsuckers** will even pound on metal signs and aluminum siding knowing that the metallic "rat-a-tat-tat" will carry farther.

Sun bathing **Western Painted Turtles** lounge on pond logs.

Dragonflies in April? First of the migrant **Common Green Darners** appear, offspring of the huge swarms that flew south last fall (see September 7-12).

Male **mosquitoes** feed on pollen. Look for their feathery antenna that separates them from the bloodthirsty females.

▲ A beautiful treasure lies hidden beneath last year's oak and basswood leaves – **Scarlet Cup Fungi.** The cup fungus with the red interior is about the diameter of a quarter and lives on the rotting fallen branches of the mature hardwood trees that tower above.

Red Maple leaves unfurl from their distinctive red bud

NORTH WOODS JOURNAL: A MINNESOTA NATURE CALENDAR

What's happenin'

A spring green flush sweeps over the landscape as **Quaking Aspen** leaves unfurl. In the common vernacular this is called "green up."

Bumblebees are buzzing about.

"Ooomp galoomp...oomp galoomp." **American Bitterns** boom from the pre-dawn depths of cattail marshes. Though rarely seen, the bittern's song is rarely forgotten.

Spring arrives on wings of blue in the form of **Spring Azure Butterflies** – tiny delicate butterflies dance along woodland trails.

If there were an *American Idol* contest for birds, the **Winter Wren** and the **Ruby-crowned Kinglet** would surely vie for top honors. Both birds are tiny but with big bubbling songs.

Massive swales of **Marsh Marigolds** blot the swampy woods with yellow.

▲ Very few trees have flowers worth admiring. But check out the gaudy red blossoms of the **Red Maple** that appear before the leaves. Also note the red bud scales and red branches. Sugar Maples have greenish flowers and will bloom in a week or two after their leaves unfurl.

Morning sun burning off the fog on the St. Louis River ❖ *Fond du Lac, St. Louis County*

NORTH WOODS JOURNAL: A MINNESOTA NATURE CALENDAR

What's happenin'

"TEACHER...TEACHER...TEACHER." The song of the **Ovenbird** rings from hardwood forests. It is not uncommon to hear three or four males singing at the same time. Ovenbirds are warblers that build domed nests that resemble old outdoor bread ovens.

Tuck your pant legs into your socks; The **Wood Ticks** are back! The first "cling-ons" can be found as early as mid-April.

Tamaracks are leafing out...or should I say "needling" out. Tiny tufts of spring green needles appear. (see photo and text for October 19-24)

Long, loud snoring calls from marshy ponds are the first signs that **Leopard Frogs** are awake. Large numbers of the spotted green-and-brown frogs are sometimes found on land.

▲ **Eastern Gray Tree Frogs** call from wooded areas. Like all tree frogs, Eastern Grays have bulbous toe pads that allow them to climb trees, walls and even smooth surfaces like windows. They can change from gray to green to match their surroundings. This guy is half and half.

Pink dawn on Lake Superior ❖ *Split Rock Lighthouse State Park*

NORTH WOODS JOURNAL: A MINNESOTA NATURE CALENDAR

What's happenin'

Like an invading French army, little noisy gulls with black heads, appropriately called **Bonaparte's Gulls**, arrive in large flocks. They were named for Charles Lucian Jules Laurent Bonaparte (younger brother of Napoleon) who was a major force in American ornithology in the 1820s.

Immense stands of **Large-flowered Trillium** carpet hardwood forests.

Sweet and gooey, the scent of opening **Balsam Poplar** buds perfumes the air. Squeeze a sticky bud and inhale the aroma. (This tree is also known as "balm of Gilead.")

Large groups of **Cliff Swallows** arrive at their preferred nesting colony sites: the undersides of highway bridges near water.

Wearing the royal colors of Lord Baltimore, orange and black **Baltimore Orioles** return.

▲ Brain-like, brown and convoluted, the **Conifer False Morel** pushes up through the dead brown leaves of the spring woods. Admire, but do not eat. A poisonous gas, methyl hydrazine, is released when cooked. Other toxins may build up in the body over time.

White Pine needles and rain drops ❖ *Nemadji River Valley, Carlton County*

NORTH WOODS JOURNAL: A MINNESOTA NATURE CALENDAR

What's happenin'

Red-bellied Snakes are one of only three species of snakes found in the North Woods, the Red-belly is a very shy and very small critter. It averages eight to ten inches long and feeds on worms, slugs, grubs and the soft parts of snails.

Red-berried Elder or **Red Elderberry** (take your pick, either name is correct) blooms.

The paper-covered buds of **spruces** will soon open to reveal tiny new needles. Gather them while still bright green for a refreshing tea.

Sandy, piney areas are where you'll find the delicate pink-blossomed and fragrant **Trailing Arbutus**.

Big-toothed Aspens are late leafers. The silvery sheen of their young leaves can be seen amidst the green of their already-leafed-out cousins, the Quaking Aspens.

▲ **Magnolia Warblers** are just one of 26 warbler species that return to the North Woods every spring. Birders travel from all over the world to see these colorful "winged jewels." Most warblers are strict insect eaters and so must winter in Mexico, Central America and South America.

Campfire in the Canoe Country ❖ *Lake Three, Boundary Waters Canoe Area Wilderness*

NORTH WOODS JOURNAL: A MINNESOTA NATURE CALENDAR

What's happenin'

Zipping back north from Mexico and Central America and straight to our gardens is everybody's favorite, the **Ruby-throated Hummingbird**. The southwestern United States has more than a dozen species.

Fruit trees of the Rose family begin blooming. **Wild Plum** first, then **Juneberry**, followed by **Pin Cherry** and finally, **Chokecherry**. Note that their showy white flowers always have five petals and many stamens.

Allegedly **American Toads** give longer calls on warmer nights. Check it out for yourself. Listen for their high-pitched trills near larger wetlands.

Bubbly-voiced **Bobolinks** return to hay fields. Like many prairie birds, Bobolinks give their mating song while in flight. In a treeless environment this gives them the visibility they need to attract a mate.

▲ **Wild Columbine** has a wonderful nickname – jester's cap. The pointed tips of the "cap" hold tiny nectaries. Some small bees and Ruby-throated Hummingbirds are able to access the sweet nectar treat but big bumbling bumble bees are shut out. Columbine often grows in rocky clefts.

A mated pair of Common Loons cruise a northern lake at sunset. They will soon raise a family together

NORTH WOODS JOURNAL: A MINNESOTA NATURE CALENDAR

What's happenin'

Common Nighthawks return to the dusk sky, swooping and gliding as they suck in airborne insects. Some have been recorded consuming 500 mosquitoes in a single night.

Whip-poor-wills incessantly call their own name. Unfortunately for light sleepers, they may keep it up all night long.

In sandy soil beneath pines look for the pink-purple flowers of **Fringed Polygala**.

White-tailed Deer fawns are odorless and lie motionless to escape detection. Somehow Black Bears find and eat a fair number.

Spiny Baskettails emerge *en masse*. Hundreds of these dragonflies swarm near lakeshores.

Interrupted Ferns are named for the stubby brown spore-bearing structures half way up the stem.

▲ It's guys' day out at the bar – the sand bar anyway. Recently emerged male **Canadian Tiger Swallowtails** gather at wet, sandy patches along roads and rivers. They sip water from the spaces between the sand grains and wait for the females to emerge. Mating will soon follow.

Falls trickle over a billion-year-old basalt lava flow ❖ *Gooseberry Falls State Park*

NORTH WOODS JOURNAL: A MINNESOTA NATURE CALENDAR

What's happenin'

Mink Frogs release a strong stench when handled. I suppose the smell reminded someone of the odor of a Mink. Their call – likened to the sound of distant knocking – can be heard in June and July.

Balsam Poplar (balm of Gilead) and **Cottonwood** trees shed "cotton." The silky-haired seeds drift from female trees to wherever the wind takes them.

The boreal forest blooms. **Twinflower**, **Bunchberry**, **Canada Mayflower** (false lily-of-the-valley), **Starflower**, **Clintonia** (bluebead lily) and **Pink Ladyslipper** (moccasin flower) are all flowering now. They are so common in the coniferous forests of the North that some nickname this group the "Canadian carpet."

Wild Leeks produce tiny but potent onionlike bulbs. Dig them now.

▲ Large, lovely mint-green **Luna Moths** show up around lights. These ephemeral beauties are living batteries, slowly running out of energy. While caterpillars, they gorged on leaves – the fuel for their winged future. Adults have no mouthparts and do not eat. Females mate, lay eggs and die.

Dock and boathouse in dawn light

NORTH WOODS JOURNAL: A MINNESOTA NATURE CALENDAR

What's happenin'

Normally quite unusual in the North Woods, **Black-billed Cuckoos** increase during the cyclic outbreaks of Eastern Forest Tent Caterpillars (see photo below).

Tiny flashes light up the night. **Fireflies**, also known as **Lightning Bugs**, are neither a fly nor a true bug, but actually a beetle. Each species not only emits its own unique sequence of flashes but the glow may be green, yellow or orange.

A most bizarre plant blooms in the floating sphagnum-moss bogs about now. **Pitcher Plant** is a carnivorous flower that lures insects to its goblet-shaped leaves and then drowns them in a deadly enzyme-rich cocktail. The insect carcass sinks to the bottom of the pitcher where special cells help the plant digest the body.

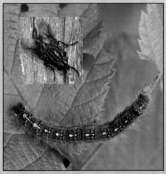

▲ Popularly known as "army worms," **Eastern Forest Tent Caterpillars** gorge on aspen leaves, often stripping whole forests. Their droppings ("frass") patter like rain as they fall from the canopy. *Sarcophagus Flies* lay their eggs in the cocoons; a natural control to a once-every-11-year event.

Moose cow getting her sodium craving satisfied by munching aquatic plants ❖ *Boundary Waters Canoe Area Wilderness*

NORTH WOODS JOURNAL: A MINNESOTA NATURE CALENDAR

What's happenin'

That's not really spit clinging to plant stems, but rather the frothy masses made by the nymphs of an insect called the **Froghopper**. The nymphs, a.k.a **Spittlebugs**, pierce the stem, suck up plant juices and blow bubbles. The yucky blob protects the developing insect until it reaches adulthood.

Clouds of yellow hang in the air on windy days as **White Pines** shed copious amounts of pollen. A golden film may coat back bays and shoreline rocks for days.

"Plunk...plunk." **Green Frogs** call from lakeshores with resounding vigor. Males have a dark green body and a bright yellow throat. Females have a white throat.

One of the few plants that is better known for its bark, **Red-osier Dogwood** also has beautiful white flowers. They are now in full bloom.

▲ Mama **Western Painted Turtles** have now left the water and are searching for soft soil or sand to lay their eggs. After digging a hole with her hind claws, mom backs in and drops 4 to 8 one-inch-long elliptical white eggs. She covers them and heads back to the safety of the water.

Lake Superior cobble beach at sunrise ❖ *Split Rock Lighthouse State Park*

NORTH WOODS JOURNAL: A MINNESOTA NATURE CALENDAR

What's happenin'

Unnoticed aliens are among us. About this time every year (to mid-July) hundreds of tiny orange butterflies congregate along dirt roads and in hay fields. They are called **European Skippers** and were introduced to North America in 1910 at London, Ontario. Since then they have spread half way across the continent. The caterpillars feast on fields of Timothy, much to the hay farmer's chagrin.

Every good Swede knows about **Lingonberries** but few know that they grow right here in the North Woods. Known locally as **Mountain Cranberry**, this close relative of the blueberry likes the cold rocky shores of Lake Superior. It blooms now and bears red fruit in August.

Shores of Lake Superior are where you'll find the gaudy purple flowers of **Beach Pea**.

▲ The stunning **Twelve-spotted Skimmer** hunts in sunny glades. Six black and white spots adorn each wing. Also check streambanks for the Ebony Jewelwing; an iridescent green damsel with black wings. Damselflies hold their wings up over their back at rest while dragonflies keep theirs spread flat.

White Water Lilies float on the reflection of a Black Spruce bog (intentionally printed upside down) ❖ *Carlton County*

NORTH WOODS JOURNAL: A MINNESOTA NATURE CALENDAR

What's happenin'

"Siamese-twin berries" are ripe in northern woods. Actually, the pair of red oblong berries that are joined at the base are the fruit of the **Northern Fly Honeysuckle**. They are not palatable.

Mountain or **Moose Maples** are now adorned with one-winged seeds (samara) designed to spin as they fall, hopefully to a fertile patch of ground.

Wolf spiders are good mothers. She attaches the egg sac with silk to her own abdomen. Soon the tiny spiderlings emerge, but they are not ready to leave home yet. Hundreds cling to mama's back as she goes about hunting.

Bristly green husks have formed around **Beaked Hazel** nuts. The husk hairs pierce and stick in human fingers but Red Squirrels are unfazed and harvest them at will.

▲ Minnesota's state flower, the **Showy Ladyslipper**, begins blooming. Two other large ladyslippers inhabit the North Woods: the Pink Ladyslipper or moccasin flower, which blooms in late May and early June in moss beds beneath spruce and pine, and the June-blooming Yellow Ladyslipper.

Bee's-eye view of Wild Lupine ❖ *North Shore of Lake Superior*

NORTH WOODS JOURNAL: A MINNESOTA NATURE CALENDAR

What's happenin'

Big, brown and beautiful, the **Polyphemus Moth** is rarely seen except when fluttering at your cabin window at night. The wings span five inches and sport bold eye-spots. It is much more common than its cousin the **Cecropia**.

Pin Cherries are ripe, and birds and chipmunks are feasting. Over 80 species of critters use this tree.

Loud, begging "cheep cheep" calls from inside a tree cavity can only mean one thing – baby **woodpeckers** are hungry and will soon fledge.

Here come the **Pine Sawyer Beetles**! The huge, slow flying insects with the insanely long antennae are out and about. Though large, they are harmless unless aggravated (i.e. pinched or pressed). It is the larval grubs of Pine Sawyers that make the creaking sound from dead and downed logs.

▲ White, fleshy, shelf-like clusters of **Oyster Mushrooms** sprout from the trunks of still-standing-but-dying aspens. They are not only edible but quite delicious when sautéed in butter. As always with wild edibles, make sure you know what you're picking before munching.

Bald Eagle so stuffed on fish that it could not fly ❖ *Athapapuskow Lake, Manitoba*

NORTH WOODS JOURNAL: A MINNESOTA NATURE CALENDAR

What's happenin'

Blueberries are now plump and juicy (in good years) or small and mealy (in bad years). Get out there with the Black Bears and grouse and pick a peck.

Moose are not the only large herbivore that enjoys munching on water lilies; **White-tailed Deer** will also partake. The high sodium content of aquatic plants make them attractive to Moose and deer.

Slime molds, contrary to the image their name imparts, are actually quite beautiful and may be pink, orange, white or chocolate brown. Watch for this tiny fungus bursting forth from rotting logs.

July is family time for **songbirds** in the North. Adult birds scramble about to feed young who have left the nest but cannot – or will not – feed themselves. The young cheep loudly as they feign helplessness.

▲ No, this is not a fungus but rather a true flowering plant. Like all wildflowers **Indian Pipe** reproduces by seed but like fungi it gets its nutrition underground so no chlorophyll is needed. The roots are in contact with a *Boletus* fungus that delivers it food directly from spruce trees.

Rainbow and White Pines ❖ *Nemadji River Valley, Carlton County*

NORTH WOODS JOURNAL: A MINNESOTA NATURE CALENDAR

What's happenin'

Sleep in! The mornings are quieter as **bird song** decreases dramatically after mid-July. Since mating season is long over and the young are out of the nest, there is no need to sing; neither to attract a mate nor to defend a territory.

Little Brown Bats forage after dark for mosquitoes and other insects. Watch one for a while. They often repeat a specific flight pattern over and over. Insects are scooped up in the tail membrane and transferred to the mouth in a split second midair maneuver.

Fire is not a bad thing in nature. A walk through a two-month-old burn reveals acres of green as **Fireweed, Large-leaved Aster, Fringed Bindweed** and **Spreading Dogbane** thrive in the sun-warmed nutrient-enriched soil. Wildlife is attracted. Eventually, aspens or pines will grow.

▲ **Cotton-grass** is neither cotton nor grass but actually a sedge. They are now very visible in the Black Spruce bogs. The Arctic Inuit, used the wooly flowering heads for wicks in their stone oil-lamps. Cotton-grasses are circumpolar – found from Canada to Scandinavia and Siberia.

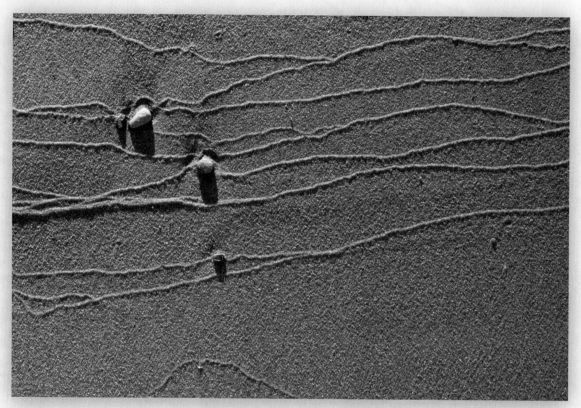

Beach pebbles and surf ripples ❖ *Minnesota Point, Duluth*

What's happenin'

Red and thimble-like, the fruits of **Thimbleberry** are starting to ripen.

"Thunk...thunk...thunk." Don't look up. **Red Squirrels** are dropping spruce cones at a rate of one every second and a half. They will cache these for winter use. Unbelievably, they are able to smell buried cones under a foot of snow!

Why are **Bald-faced Hornets** capturing mosquitoes and flies? They haul them back to the hive where they chew them up and feed them to the developing larvae. In return they get to eat the sugary "honeydew" regurgitated by the larvae.

Check Ox-eye Daisy, Brown-eyed Susan and goldenrod flower heads for the ambushing **Goldenrod Crab Spider**. They are even able to change from yellow-to-white or white-to-yellow to match the flower they are hunting on.

▲ Second-summer **Black Bears** are now on their own; Mom has made that quite plain. Two to three eight-ounce young are born to a snoozing mom in the winter den. The chipmunk-sized cubs crawl to a teet and begin suckling. They will put on six pounds before emerging in spring.

Orange Hawkweed amidst native and alien roadside flowers ❖ *Carlton County*

North Woods Journal: A Minnesota Nature Calendar

What's happenin'

Sad, but true; migration is now beginning. Flocks of **shorebirds** and **Common Grackles** are already moving south. Amazingly, your local sewage ponds are probably the best place to see migrating **sandpipers**, **plovers**, **yellowlegs** and **dowitchers**.

August has been "berry, berry good to me." Though strawberries are done, about everything else is ripe. **Thimbleberries, raspberries, blueberries, gooseberries, skunk currants, pin cherries** and **juneberries** are all available for the picking.

Bunchberries are all bunched up, round, ripe and red. Grouse seek them out...as do some humans. Try a couple. Pop a few in your mouth and suck on them. I find them a refreshing treat while on the trail. Careful, each has a rather large stone in the center.

▲ Golden yellow **Chanterelles** push up through pine needle duff. Search for this excellent edible mushroom under pines during early to mid-August, especially after wet spells. It is a much-utilized fungus in Europe where it is dried and sold in camping stores.

Fungi working to digest a rotting tree ❖ *Oberg Mountain, Cook County*

What's happenin'

Small family groups of **Cedar Waxwings** give soft, high-pitched trills as they forage for berries.

Some birds may still be sitting on eggs. **Eastern Phoebes** and **American Robins** commonly have a second brood in late summer.

American Goldfinches delay nesting until thistles have gone to seed. Down is gathered by the "wild canaries" and carefully placed as a lining in their nests.

Signs of fall already? **Bracken Ferns** begin yellowing (see photo Aug. 19-24). The entire plant will turn brown with the first hard frosts.

"Summer is over when **Fireweed** blooms to the top," the saying goes. Purple buds open into purple flowers from the bottom up, finally reaching the top of the flower spike in late summer.

▲ Mistakenly called "wolf spiders," the huge, long-legged spiders found on cabin walls, docks and outbuildings are actually **Dark Fishing Spiders** (*Dolomedes tennebrosus*). Females may have a four-inch legspan. They are also found near lakeshores where they will dive for minnows.

Gooseberry Falls and the first hint of fall color ❖ *Gooseberry Falls State Park*

NORTH WOODS JOURNAL: A MINNESOTA NATURE CALENDAR

What's happenin'

Fuzzy white growths on **Speckled Alder** are not plants at all but large clusters of insects called **Wooly Alder Aphids**. The "wool" is actually a mass of waxy filaments extruded through pores on their back. The aphids feed on alder sap and in turn may be preyed on by the carnivorous caterpillars of **Harvester butterflies**.

Waves of warblers begin moving south. Most are now in drab fall plumage and thus complicating identification.

Blue Jays are excellent mimics. I once heard a jay perform a perfect Broad-winged Hawk whistle.

White-lined Sphinx Moths do a pretty good impression of a hummingbird as they hover near garden flowers at dusk.

Spreading Dogbane leaves are now yellow and drooping.

▲ **Fly Amanita** mushrooms are up. It is wise to consider this forest beauty a deadly poison. Raiding Vikings were said to get a burst of superhuman strength from eating the European version of this fungus. Unfortunately, death was a common and permanent side effect.

Autumn is just around the corner; Bracken Ferns turn yellow ❖ *Superior Hiking Trail, North Shore*

NORTH WOODS JOURNAL: A MINNESOTA NATURE CALENDAR

What's happenin'

Like the Energizer Bunny, **Red-eyed Vireos** sing on...and on...and on.

Minnesota **Monarchs** begin their awesome 2000-mile migration to the mountains of central Mexico. Their offspring will return to the North Woods next spring. In January 1976, Dr. Fred Urquhart picked up a Monarch in Mexico that had been tagged by Jim Gilbert at the Minnesota Landscape Arboretum on September 6, 1975. This proved that northern Monarchs do fly all the way to Mexico.

August was made for **grasshoppers**. They seem to be everywhere. Minnesota has more than 100 species of grasshoppers, katydids and crickets.

Small red dragonflies are active now through late September. They are members of the genus *Sympetrum* – the **meadowhawks**.

▲ "Oh, what symmetric webs they weave," or some saying like that. But it is true of the *Araneus* orbweaver spiders. Watch for their large, stereotypical webs in wooded areas, under eaves of buildings, on street signs, mailboxes, etc. They are often large spiders with a bulbous abdomen.

A Sugar Maple leaf has fallen to its final resting place – a bed of Haircap Moss ❖ *Banning State Park, Pine County*

NORTH WOODS JOURNAL: A MINNESOTA NATURE CALENDAR

What's happenin'

Hundreds, even thousands, of migrating **Common Nighthawks** stream south on certain sunny warm evenings an hour or two before sunset. An astounding 43,690 were recorded in Duluth on August 26, 1990.

Wild Rice is ripe in the marshy bays of shallow lakes. **Virginia Rails** are common in the thickest stands. The Ojibwa knew them as "rice birds," guardians of the rice. Pale **long-jawed orbweaver spiders** are also abundant. Wild Rice was an Ojibwa food staple for centuries and still is an import native commodity.

A few **Sugar Maple** leaves turn shades of yellow, red or orange.

Red Baneberry fruits can be either red or white ("doll's-eyes"). **White Baneberry** also produces white berries but they are attached to the stalk with thick red peduncles.

▲ **Goldenrods** are late-blooming flowers that attract late-season insects. **Goldenrod Soldier Beetles** are common now. Nine species of goldenrods bloom in late summer meadows around the North Woods. Zigzag Goldenrod, though, defies its family's sun-loving lineage and blooms in shady woods.

River ripples reflect fall foliage, blue sky and birch trunks ❖ *Temperence River State Park*

NORTH WOODS JOURNAL: A MINNESOTA NATURE CALENDAR

What's happenin'

Large blue and green dragonflies called darners are common during early September. Fifteen species are active now including **Canada Darners**, **Common Green Darners**, **Lake Darners**, **Black-tipped Darners** and even rare **Zigzag Darners**.

Any day now we could experience the first **killing frost** of fall.

Velvet is being shed from the antlers of buck **White-tailed Deer**. A bush or small sapling is thrashed repeatedly over several hours to remove the skin. The deer may even eat its own shed velvet.

Step outside on a calm, clear night and just listen. If it is quiet, you may hear the "tweets, chips and squeaks" of thousands of birds flying overhead. **Warblers**, **sparrows** and **thrushes** all migrate at night using the stars as their compass.

▲ **Tiger beetles** are ferocious insect predators. If they were the size of golden retrievers we'd all be in trouble. Pick a warm mid-September day and carefully scan any sandy lakeshore or dune for movement. Old gravel pits are also a favorite haunt of these striking beetles.

Falls on the Temperence River ❖ *Temperence River State Park*

NORTH WOODS JOURNAL: A MINNESOTA NATURE CALENDAR

What's happenin'

Franklin's Ground Squirrels are fattening up for their long sleep.

Scarlet red **Virginia Creeper** leaves stand out against the browns of the tree trunks to which they cling.

Eastern Bluebirds are flocking up but lingering. They are feeding on late-season insects before they head south to the southern states and Mexico.

Free lemonade! Bite off a mouthful of **sumac** berries and suck on them. The tart hairs make a refreshing treat. When you are done, simply spit out the seeds.

Black Bears must put on a 100 pound layer of fat before denning up for the winter. Dogwood berries and acorns are late season staples. It is believed bears will travel up to 100 miles to find an especially productive stand of oaks.

▲ **Common Green Darners** move south in huge numbers every fall. Estimates have topped 30,000 in a day at Duluth's Hawk Ridge. Migrating at the same time, American Kestrels snag green darners out of the air, plucking the dragonfly's wings off in midflight before eating them.

Dew drops on Big-toothed Aspen leaf ❖ *North Shore of Lake Superior*

NORTH WOODS JOURNAL: A MINNESOTA NATURE CALENDAR

What's happenin'

Every fall a few **Parasitic Jaegers** stop by Lake Superior on their way to wintering waters in the Atlantic Ocean. The large gull-like birds from the Arctic specialize in terrorizing gulls into dropping their catch.

Divergent Metallic Wood-Borers cling to dying pine trunks. The football-shaped 3/4-inch-long beetle is shiny bronze. Larva bore into stems, roots and logs.

High pressure with northwest winds and blue skies equals massive movements of **Broad-winged Hawks**. A phenomenal 101,698 were tallied over Duluth's Hawk Ridge on September 15, 2003.

Large, loose flocks of **Blue Jays** wing their way south. How far south? Some jays from Canada may stop in northern Minnesota while others may end up in Texas.

▲ As the leaves begin to fall, we notice abandoned hives of **Bald-faced Hornets**. The large black and white bees scrape rotting wood and mix it with their saliva to make a type of paper – the material for their hives. Paper Wasps, by contrast, are black and yellow and make underground nests.

Kettle River flowing past sandstone ledges ❖ *Banning State Park, Pine County*

NORTH WOODS JOURNAL: A MINNESOTA NATURE CALENDAR

What's happenin'

Fireweed often colonizes newly burned, bombed or bulldozed landscapes. Its feathery seeds drift on the wind to areas of bare soil.

Totally orange, completely yellow or red with yellow veins...**Big-toothed Aspen** leaves are quite variable in color but always have big "teeth" along their margins. Their leaves begin falling in late September.

Northern Flickers seek out ripe **Virginia Creeper** berries. This energy-rich food will help them make it to their wintering grounds.

Basswood leaves are now yellow, and a good wind will shake some free.

Swamp-loving **Black Ash** are nearly the last trees to sprout leaves in spring yet the first to lose them in the fall. Many ashes are already bare-branch naked.

▲ A "robber's mask" helps identify the **Wood Frog**, which will soon hunker down beneath leaf litter for the winter. As they slowly freeze solid, their heart will stop. Come spring, they thaw out, the heart pumps and off they jump. Glycerol, nature's antifreeze, makes this possible.

Black Spruce, White Spruce and Sugar Maple ❖ *Oberg Mountain, Cook County*

NORTH WOODS JOURNAL: A MINNESOTA NATURE CALENDAR

What's happenin'

Maple fruits (samara) litter the ground and **Eastern Gray Squirrels** are opportunistically eating the seeds and discarding the "wing."

Yellow-rumped Warblers and **Palm Warblers** are everywhere! Many are feeding along roads where the warm pavement attracts late-season insects.

Snow commonly falls in late September, but does not stick.

Even though they hatched out four months ago, juvenile **Common Loons** are still begging for food. Occasionally mom and dad give in and stuff a fish down junior's throat. Some adult Common Loons are now in their drab winter plumage while others still sport the black and white. Large flocks assemble on bigger lakes before migrating to the Gulf Coast and Atlantic Seaboard.

▲ **Wooly Bear Caterpillars** fatten up on plantain leaves before looking for a safe place to hibernate. Next summer they will transform into a white or yellow Isabella Moth. Wooly Bears were once thought to predict the severity of the coming winter by the width of their golden brown band.

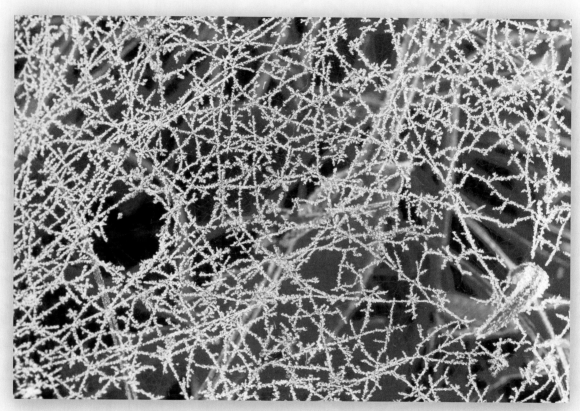

Frost on the web of an Agelenopsis Grass Spider ❖ *Carlton County*

NORTH WOODS JOURNAL: A MINNESOTA NATURE CALENDAR

What's happenin'

After dark, hundreds of **Saw-whet Owls** are moving down the North Shore. Over 130 were banded in a single night at Duluth's Hawk Ridge on October 5, 1993.

Most wildflowers are long gone, but a few **Large-leaved Asters** are still in bloom.

Ballooning silk clings to weed stalks and tree branches. Young spiders (**spiderlings**) shoot out a thread of silk and ride the wind as they disperse to new areas.

European Starlings and **American Robins** continue gorging on over-ripe **Chokecherries**.

Sugar Maple leaves are near peak. The treetops that are more exposed to sunlight turn first. Maples on the highlands above Lake Superior peak earlier than the birch and aspen on the North Shore.

▲ **Staghorn Sumac** leaves are a stunning study in scarlet. Their branches are covered with fine hairs like the velvet on a "stag" deer's antlers. Red Oaks are just now showing nice color. In contrast, the leaves of Black Ash and American Basswood are already on the ground.

Migrating Canada Geese rest on a pool of reflected fall color ❖ *Rock Pond, University of Minnesota, Duluth*

NORTH WOODS JOURNAL: A MINNESOTA NATURE CALENDAR

What's happenin'

Quaking Aspen (a.k.a. trembling aspen, poplar, popal) is the dominant tree over much of the North Woods and now is their time to shine. Yellow paints the landscape with a broad brush as aspen color peaks.

Highbush Cranberry fruits ripened in September but they are still clinging to the trees. The hanging clusters of red berries are eaten by 34 species of birds and mammals. This is an especially important shrub to wildlife as its berries persist into winter.

A new scourge in the North – the **Asian Ladybird Beetle** – invades our homes as they search for a place to hibernate. Introduced to the East Coast in the late 1970s to control aphids, they have spread across the continent, reaching Minnesota in the mid 1990s.

▲ Some autumns produce a bumper crop of **Mountain Ash berries** much to the delight of catbirds, thrashers, robins, thrushes and waxwings. Two native species inhabit the North Woods. Known as the "rowan tree" in Europe, it was once planted near doorways to keep away evil spirits.

Green all summer, Blueberry leaves now turn crimson ❖ *Minnesota Point, Duluth*

NORTH WOODS JOURNAL: A MINNESOTA NATURE CALENDAR

What's happenin'

Bunchberry leaves have become deep purple with age.

Find any weedy patch this time of fall and it is sure to be full of sparrows. Good areas can easily produce a half dozen species and ten is not out of the question. The skulking sparrows feed on grass and weed seeds. Most common will probably be **Dark-eyed Juncos, American Tree, Savannah, White-throated, White-crowned, Fox, Song, Harris's** and **Lincoln's Sparrows.**

Sandhill Cranes soar and wheel overhead on their way to wintering grounds in New Mexico's Bosque del Apache National Wildlife Refuge via the Platte River in Nebraska. They breed in brushy wetlands from Hudson Bay south to central Minnesota and southern Wisconsin.

▲ Every ten years or so, **Northern Goshawks** make large movements south in search of food. These irruptions are probably related to the population cycles of their prey: Snowshoe Hares and Ruffed Grouse. Mid-October is the peak of the goshawk flight over Duluth's Hawk Ridge.

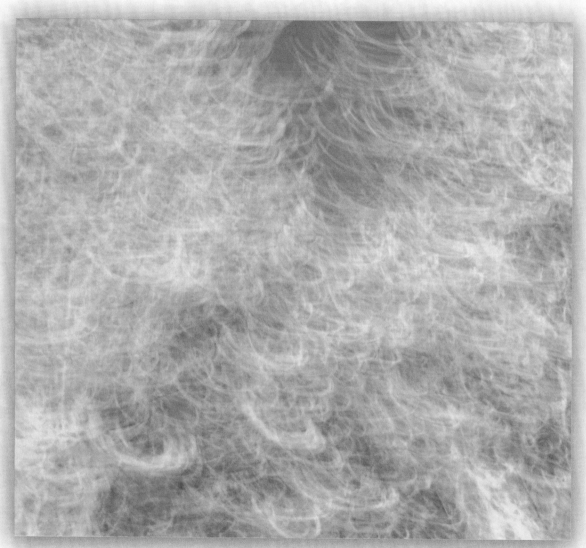

Smoky-gold Tamaracks sway in a stiff autumn breeze ❖ *Sax-Zim Bog, St. Louis County*

NORTH WOODS JOURNAL: A MINNESOTA NATURE CALENDAR

What's happenin'

Tamaracks turn a splendid "smoky gold." The trees will lose their needles before the end of October.

A flurry of white-winged birds flying up from the roadside are sure to be **Snow Buntings**, small sparrow-like birds that nest on the tundra of northern Canada and winter from southern Minnesota to northern Kansas and Missouri.

Lake Superior's North Shore is a major funnel for migrating song-birds. Counts from August through October revealed a movement of over a quarter million birds each fall. More than 19,000 **American Robins** were recorded heading south in October 1994.

Don't be surprised to wake up to "shovelable" white stuff. We often get our first **measurable snow** in mid- to late October.

▲ Large flocks of **Snow Geese** (including some of the blue color morph) pierce October's blue skies. The dark morph was formerly thought to be a separate species called the "Blue Goose." Huge numbers winter at Bosque del Apache National Wildlife Refuge in New Mexico.

Mountain Ash berry clusters cling to bare branches ❖ *North Shore of Lake Superior*

North Woods Journal: A Minnesota Nature Calendar

What's happenin'

Pale, delicate moths called **Linden Loopers** flutter about cabin windows after dark. They seem to be the only insect left flying about the woods.

Shaggy Mane mushrooms pop up after wet weather. Other late season fungi include the diminutive **Eyelash Cup** (a tiny orange saucer rimmed with black "hairs", found on logs) and **Blue Stain** (tiny blue stalked cups on pieces of rotten wood stained blue-green by their "roots" called mycelia).

Just like deciduous trees, **pines, spruces and firs** lose their leaves every fall. Each needle lives three or four years, turns brown and then falls off. Evergreens are only "ever green" because this rotation means that there are always two or three years' worth of green needles on the tree at any one time.

▲ "The fridge ain't gonna fill itself," the **Beavers** seem to be saying as they dutifully drop trees (they can gnaw down a six-inch-diameter tree in 15 minutes) and clip branches to stash in an underwater cache. This stockpile will hopefully feed the entire family until ice-out in spring.

A lone Ground–Pine Club Moss in a Bunchberry patch ❖ *Oberg Mountain, Cook County*

NORTH WOODS JOURNAL: A MINNESOTA NATURE CALENDAR

What's happenin'

Cold November gales scatter **cattail** seeds as the hotdog-shaped heads fall apart.

Muskrats have mostly finished their dome-shaped houses. Last minute cattails are being added to their middle-of-the-marsh dwellings.

Long-tailed Ducks (formerly known as Oldsquaws) congregate in large "rafts" on Lake Superior, especially around Grand Marais, Minnesota.

Not much is green in the woods right now, so colonies of **club moss** stand out. Also known as ground pines or princess pines, club mosses are neither young pines nor mosses but members of the genus *Lycopodium*. Flick a spore head in late fall to create a tiny yellow cloud of shed spores. The spores ignite easily and were once used to create the "flash" for early photographers.

▲ **Wintergreen** leaves contain oil of wintergreen and when crushed, smell just like Wintergreen Certs. The red berries cling to plants through the winter, if not comandeered by Spruce Grouse or chipmunks, and make a pleasant nibble come spring.

A wary Coyote comes in to snatch a rabbit carcass when it spies a competitor — another hungry Coyote

What's happenin'

Ponds and small lakes freeze over. Feeding flocks of ducks and geese can maintain pockets of open water for a while.

Hunting over open fields are tundra-breeding **Rough-legged Hawks.** They have moved south in search of snow-free fields filled with mice. Note their wide black belly band and black patches under the wings.

The **White-tailed Deer** rut is on – and so is deer hunting season.

Clear, blue-sky days with northwest winds are the perfect conditions for flights of **Bald Eagles.** This southward push is less of a migration than a movement in search of food. Many eagles will stay the winter in the North feeding on road-killed deer while others winter along the Mississippi River where open water means fishing opportunities. Keep your eyes on the sky!

▲ The gales of November toss up tons of new rock material onto Lake Superior's beaches, including Minnesota's state gemstone – the **Lake Superior Agate**. Formed by mineral-rich waters crystallizing inside petrified gas bubbles, agates were later knocked out of basalt bedrock by glaciers.

Auraora borealis and stars. Winter is the best time to see the northern lights ❖ *Athapapuskow Lake, Manitoba*

NORTH WOODS JOURNAL: A MINNESOTA NATURE CALENDAR

What's happenin'

Snowshoe Hares are not the only critters to turn white in winter (see photo below). **Short-tailed** and **Long-tailed Weasels** become completely white except for a black-tipped tail. **Least Weasels** turn totally white. Weasels not only change pelage in winter, they also change names; they are now called "ermine."

A blizzard of white and black swirls up from wind-whipped fields. **Snow Buntings** feed on fallen grass seeds in large flocks; then when one jumps, the whole flock flies. They wheel and bank in formation until it is determined the coast is clear, whereupon they land and keep on feeding. Deeper snows in the North Woods force them south to the agricultural fields of southern Minnesota and Iowa. One even reached Texas a few years back.

▲ Transformation: **Snowshoe Hares** are in the midst of their slow turn from brown to white. In a perfect world they would complete the color change just as the first snows of winter blanketed the ground; then their camouflage would be complete.

Trio of Paper Birch in field of Red Osier Dogwood ❖ *Nemadji River Valley*

NORTH WOODS JOURNAL: A MINNESOTA NATURE CALENDAR

What's happenin'

Have you ever seen a cluster of **Northern White Cedars** that seemed to have been neatly trimmed up to about six feet? This is the work of browsing **White-tailed Deer** who love to eat cedar. They need about six to eight pounds of browse per day. Sugar Maple, Basswood and Red-osier Dogwood are other favorites.

Milkweed is as distinctive now as when it was blooming in July. Large warty seedpods that are pointed at one end and rounded on the other have split open and are shedding white feathery seeds across windswept meadows.

Mature buck **deer** thrash specific small trees with their antlers. Scents from glands on their forehead are also rubbed into the spot. This action declares to other bucks, "I was here and I intend to stay here."

▲ **Hoar frost** is a spectacular late fall phenomenon that creates postcard perfect photo opportunities. On absolutely calm nights, delicate feathery ice crystals form on objects that are colder than 32 degrees Fahrenheit (bare branches, seed pods, leaves, fences, etc.).

Ice-covered bush after a November storm ❖ *Stoney Point, North Shore*

NORTH WOODS JOURNAL: A MINNESOTA NATURE CALENDAR

What's happenin'

Most northern **lakes are now frozen** shore to shore. Safe snowshoeing, skating, ice fishing and polka dancing on area lakes requires four inches of ice.

Vertical pinecones appear to tip some willow branches. Each is actually the work of a gnat that laid her eggs in a willow's terminal bud. The plant responded just as the gnat wanted, by growing this **willow-cone gall** that will protect the larvae until they emerge as adults next spring.

Raccoons are seeking hollow trees and vacant outbuildings for their long winter sleep. They are not true hibernators and will awake during warm winter days.

The **gales of November** can result in massive waves on Lake Superior. Shoreline plants are sometimes encased in ice (see photo left).

▲ **Moose** thrash their antlers on innocent saplings each fall to rid themselves of the velvet that supplied the developing antlerbone with blood. Now, during the rut, they use "rubs" to signpost to other Moose that they are the dominant bull in the area.

Winter camping under a full moon at minus 30 degrees (in-camera double exposure) ❖ *Quetico Provincial Park, Ontario*

NORTH WOODS JOURNAL: A MINNESOTA NATURE CALENDAR

What's happenin'

Winter is not lifeless – though much of that life is hidden. Millions of critters are hibernating all around us: **insect larvae**, some adult **butterflies**, **Wooly Bear Caterpillars**, **frogs**, **salamanders**, **Western Painted Turtles**, **Snapping Turtles**, **Eastern Garter Snakes**, **Red-bellied Snakes**, four species of **bats**, **Least Chipmunks**, **Eastern Chipmunks**, **Woodchucks**, **Franklin's Ground Squirrels** and **Black Bears**.

Flashes of lightning and claps of thunder during a winter snow-storm? It is possible but quite rare. This weather phenomenon is called **"thunder snow."**

American Goldfinches are no longer gold. Their winter plumage is drab yellow and gray. Goldfinches are common at northern thistle feeders some years but absent other winters.

▲ Watch for the wandering flocks of **Bohemian Waxwings** that descend on areas with fruit-laden Mountain Ashes or crab apples. Like other irruptive species, Bohemian Waxwings wander in search of food. When they strip the trees of fruit, they move on.

Silence in the valley. Spruces, snow and Lost Lake ❖ *Jay Cooke State Park, Carlton County*

What's happenin'

Birch seeds drifting down from the canopy are a sure sign that a flock of **Common Redpolls** is feeding overhead. The fleur-de-lis-shaped seeds are a favorite of these tiny red-capped finches. A true circumpolar species, Common Redpolls breed in Scandinavia, Siberia, Alaska and northern Canada.

Have you ever tried "pishing?" Make the hushing sound you would make to a noisy child in the library. Now draw it out for three to five seconds, and at regular intervals close your lips. Repeat this loudly. **Black-capped Chickadees** pish in quite easily, as will **Red-breasted Nuthatches, White-breasted Nuthatches and Downy Woodpeckers**. Occasionally you will get a big surprise as I did when a **Pine Marten** appeared from the spruces to check out the mystery sound.

▲ Drive any country road at dusk on a calm clear cold night and you will most likely see the silhouettes of one or more **Ruffed Grouse** in the tops of Quaking Aspens. They gorge themselves on buds and then dive under the snow to sleep the night in relative warmth and safety.

A tiny Common Redpoll fluffs out its feathers to stay warm ❖ *Duluth*

NORTH WOODS JOURNAL: A MINNESOTA NATURE CALENDAR

What's happenin'

Nighttime visitors to your sunflower feeder may include the cute **Northern Flying Squirrel**. Its cuteness is partially derived from its large eyes, a necessary feature for a strictly nocturnal animal. While they sit at the feeder, note the loose flaps of skin between the front and hind legs. This is their built-in parasail. Scampering up a nearby tree, they launch themselves with legs spread wide. The extra skin cape allows them to glide 30 to 130 feet between trees. During the day they curl up with others in hollow trees lined with leaves, mosses, feathers and tree bark. Their diet away from the feeder includes tree buds, flowers, fruits, seeds, fungi, insects, bird eggs and nestlings. Surprisingly, flying squirrels are likely the most abundant squirrel in forested parts of Minnesota.

▲ Fungus is a rare sight in December, but clinging faithfully to birch trunks is the perennial **Birch Conk**. Note the raised ridges of each year's new growth of spore tubes. Voyageurs soaked chunks of this "tinder polypore" in a saltpeter solution to catch the sparks from their flint and steel.

Lake Superior on a calm winter day ❖ *Stoney Point, North Shore*

NORTH WOODS JOURNAL: A MINNESOTA NATURE CALENDAR

What's happenin'

A lack of microtynes (mice and voles) in the boreal forests of Canada will force day-hunting **Great Gray Owls** and **Northern Hawk-Owls** south into northern Minnesota. In December 1995 the Sax-Zim Christmas Bird Count (30 miles northwest of Duluth) recorded an exceptional 28 Great Gray Owls in a 15-mile diameter circle!

What booms like nearby thunder, cracks like a shotgun blast and groans and creaks like a giant leaning pine? The answer is **lake ice** as it expands during the day and contracts at night.

Pick a day after a light dusting of snow and **go tracking**. Wet snow preserves track details. Little-used dirt roads, lake ice and the ground near feeders are good places to check for the paw prints and hoof prints of winter-active critters.

▲ **Moose** crave salt. Because of their dietary preference they will kneel down on salted roads to lick up this winter snack. But obviously, their mobility is greatly impaired by the awkward kneeling position, making them a real road hazard to northland drivers.

Staghorn Sumac after a snow squall ❖ *Carlton County*

NORTH WOODS JOURNAL: A MINNESOTA NATURE CALENDAR

What's happenin'

White-tailed Deer and **Moose** have antlers not horns. Antlers are bone and are shed every year in winter. Horns (bison, cattle) are made up of modified hairs and are permanent. Deer and Moose start to drop their antlers this time of year though I have seen antlered Moose well into March.

Leaves of **Northern Red Oak** and **White Oak** still cling to branches, lonely and rattling in the cold winter winds.

Step outside on a clear night and search the north sky for displays of the **aurora borealis**, or Northern Lights (see photo Nov. 13-18). The glowing bands, waves and curtains of green – or red if you're really lucky – are the result of solar flares, which send highly charged particles towards the magnetic poles that then react with oxygen and nitrogen atoms.

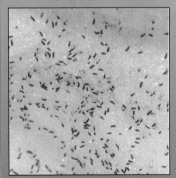

▲ Like pepper specks on the snow, **Springtails** (**Snow Fleas**) congregate on warm winter days. The wingless insects propel themselves by releasing a spring-loaded appendage. While only 3 mm long, they can jump 3 inches. If humans could leap this far, the world record for long jump would be 150 feet!

Sunrise & Sunset Table

All times are Central Standard Time and have been adjusted for daylight savings time which begins on the first Sunday in April and ends the last Sunday in October (yellow shaded area).

	Duluth	Grand Marais	Ely	Grand Rapids	Bemidji	Brainerd
January 1	7:53am/4:29pm	7:50am/4:18pm	7:57am/4:24pm	8:00am/4:33pm	8:07am/4:37pm	8:00am/4:40pm
January 10	7:52am/4:38pm	7:48am/4:27pm	7:55am/4:33pm	7:59am/4:42pm	8:05am/4:47pm	7:59am/4:50pm
January 20	7:46am/4:51pm	7:42am/4:41pm	7:49am/4:47pm	7:53am/4:56pm	7:59am/5:00pm	7:53am/5:03pm
February 1	7:34am/5:09pm	7:29am/4:59pm	7:36am/5:05pm	7:40am/5:14pm	7:47am/5:18pm	7:41am/5:21pm
February 10	7:21am/5:23pm	7:17am/5:13pm	7:23am/5:19pm	7:28am/5:27pm	7:34am/5:32pm	7:29am/5:34pm
February 20	7:06am/5:38pm	7:00am/5:29pm	7:07am/5:35pm	7:12am/5:43pm	7:18am/5:48pm	7:13am/5:49am
March 1	6:48am/5:53pm	6:42am/5:45pm	6:48am/5:51pm	6:54am/5:58pm	7:00am/6:03pm	6:55am/6:04pm
March 10	6:31am/6:06pm	6:24am/5:58pm	6:30am/6:04pm	6:36am/6:11pm	6:42am/6:17pm	6:38am/6:16pm
March 20	6:11am/6:20pm	6:04am/6:13pm	6:10am/6:19pm	6:17am/6:25pm	6:22am/6:31pm	6:19am/6:30pm
April 1	5:47am/6:36pm	5:39am/6:30pm	5:46am/6:36pm	5:53am/6:42pm	5:58am/6:48pm	5:56am/6:46pm
April 10	6:30am/7:49pm	6:21am/7:43pm	6:28am/7:49pm	6:35am/7:55pm	6:40am/8:01pm	6:38am/7:58pm
April 20	6:11am/8:02pm	6:02am/7:57pm	6:08am/8:04pm	6:16am/8:09pm	6:21am/8:15pm	6:20am/8:12pm
May 1	5:53am/8:17pm	5:43am/8:13pm	5:49am/8:19pm	5:57am/8:24pm	6:02am/8:30pm	6:02am/8:26pm
May 10	5:40am/8:29pm	5:29am/8:25pm	5:35am/8:32pm	5:44am/8:36pm	5:49am/8:42pm	5:49am/8:38pm
May 20	5:27am/8:41pm	5:17am/8:38pm	5:23am/8:44pm	5:32am/8:48pm	5:36am/8:55pm	5:37am/8:50pm
June 1	5:17am/8:54pm	5:06am/8:51pm	5:12am/8:58pm	5:21am/9:01pm	5:26am/9:08pm	5:28am/9:02pm
June 10	5:14am/9:01pm	5:02am/8:58pm	5:08am/9:05pm	5:18am/9:08pm	5:22am/9:15pm	5:24am/9:08pm
June 20	5:13am/9:05pm	5:02am/9:03pm	5:08am/9:10pm	5:17am/9:13pm	5:22am/9:20pm	5:24am/9:13pm
July 1	5:18am/9:06pm	5:06am/9:03pm	5:12am/9:10pm	5:22am/9:13pm	5:26am/9:20pm	5:29am/9:12pm
July 10	5:24am/9:02pm	5:13am/8:59pm	5:19am/9:06pm	5:28am/9:09pm	5:33am/9:16pm	5:35am/9:09pm
July 20	5:34am/8:55pm	5:23am/8:51pm	5:29am/8:58pm	5:38am/9:02pm	5:43am/9:08pm	5:45am/9:01pm
August 1	5:48am/8:41pm	5:37am/8:37am	5:44am/8:43pm	5:52am/8:47pm	5:57am/8:54pm	5:59am/8:47pm
August 10	5:59am/8:27pm	5:49am/8:23pm	5:55am/8:30pm	6:04am/8:34pm	6:08am/8:40pm	6:10am/8:33pm
August 20	6:12am/8:11pm	6:03am/8:06pm	6:09am/8:12pm	6:17am/8:17am	6:22am/8:23pm	6:22am/8:17pm
September 1	6:27am/7:48pm	6:19am/7:43pm	6:25am/7:49pm	6:33am/7:55pm	6:38am/8:01pm	6:38am/7:55pm
September 10	6:39am/7:31pm	6:31am/7:24pm	6:37am/7:31pm	6:44am/7:37pm	6:50am/7:43pm	6:49am/7:37pm
September 20	6:52am/7:11pm	6:45am/7:04pm	6:51am/7:10pm	6:58am/7:16pm	7:03am/7:22pm	7:02am/7:17pm
October 1	7:07am/6:49pm	7:00am/6:41pm	7:06am/6:47pm	7:12am/6:54pm	7:18am/7:00pm	7:16am/6:56pm
October 10	7:19am/6:31pm	7:12am/6:23pm	7:19am/6:29pm	7:25am/6:36pm	7:31am/6:42pm	7:28am/6:39pm
October 20	7:33am/6:13pm	7:27am/6:04pm	7:34am/6:10pm	7:39am/6:18pm	7:45am/6:23pm	7:42am/6:21pm
November 1	6:50am/4:53pm	6:45am/4:43pm	6:52am/4:50pm	6:57am/4:58pm	7:03am/5:03pm	6:59am/5:01pm
November 10	7:03am/4:40pm	6:59am/4:30pm	7:06am/4:37pm	7:10am/4:45pm	7:16am/4:50pm	7:12am/4:49pm
November 20	7:18am/4:29pm	7:14am/4:19pm	7:20am/4:25pm	7:25am/4:34pm	7:31am/4:38pm	7:26am/4:39pm
December 1	7:32am/4:22pm	7:29am/4:11pm	7:35am/4:17pm	7:39am/4:26pm	7:46am/4:30pm	7:40am/4:32pm
December 10	7:42am/4:19pm	7:39am/4:08pm	7:45am/4:14pm	7:49am/4:23pm	7:56am/4:28pm	7:50am/4:30pm
December 20	7:49am/4:21pm	7:46am/4:10pm	7:53am/4:16pm	7:57am/4:25pm	8:03am/4:30pm	7:57am/4:33pm

Full Moon Dates

A "blue moon" is the second full moon in a single month. As you can see from the chart below this once-in-a-blue-moon event will happen in May 2007, December 2009 and August 2012. Check your local paper or the internet for actual rising times.

	2005	2006	2007	2008	2009	2010	2011	2012	2013	2014	2015
January	25	14	3	22	10	30	19	9	26	15	4
February	23	12	1	20	9	28	18	7	25	14	3
March	25	14	3	21	10	29	19	8	27	16	5
April	24	13	2	20	9	28	17	6	25	15	4
May	23	13	2/31	19	8	27	17	5	24	14	3
June	21	11	30	18	7	26	15	4	23	12	2
July	21	10	29	18	7	25	15	3	22	12	1
August	19	9	28	16	5	24	13	1/31	20	10	31
September	17	7	26	15	4	23	12	29	19	8	29
October	17	6	25	14	4	22	11	29	18	8	27
November	15	5	24	13	2	21	10	28	17	6	25
December	15	4	23	12	2/31	21	10	28	17	6	25

Photo Credits

Ryan Marshik (rsmarshik@duluth.com): January 1-6, 25-31, February 13-18, March 7-12, April 1-6, May 1-6, 13-18, 25-31, June 1-6, 7-12, 13-18, 19-24, 25-30, July 13-18, August 7-12, 19-24, 25-31, September 1-6, 7-12, 19-24, 25-30, November 7-12, 13-18, December 1-6, 13-18, 19-24.

Sparky Stensaas (sparkystensaas@hotmail.com): All right-page sidebar photos, January 7-12, 13-18, 19-24, February 1-6, 7-12, 19-24, 25-29, March 1-6, 13-18, 19-24, 25-31, April 7-12, 13-18, 19-24, 25-30, May 7-12, 19-24, July 1-6, 7-12, 19-24, 25-31, August 1-6, 13-18, September 13-18, October 1-6, 7-12, 13-18, 19-24, 25-31, November 1-6, 19-24, 25-30, December 7-12, 25-31.

All photos in this book are available as matted prints. Prices are subject to change. Please e-mail the photographer with your requests.

$60 for a 8x10-inch photo with 11x14-inch white mat; shrink wrapped.
$80 for a 11x14-inch photo with 14x17 white mat; shrink wrapped.

Index

a

acorns: September 7-12
agate, Lake Superior: November 7-12
Alder, Speckled: April 19-24, August 13-18
Amanita, Fly: August 13-18
American Basswood: October 1-6, November 19-24
American Bittern: May 1-6
American Crow: March 25-31
American Goldfinch: August 7-12, December 1-6
American Kestrel: September 7-12
American Robin: March 25-31, August 7-12, October 1-6, 19-24
American Toad: May 25-31
Amercian Tree Sparrow: October 13-18
American Woodcock: April 7-12
antlers: January 25-31, September 1-6, November 19-24, 25-30, December 25-31
Ant, Carpenter: February 25-29
Aphid, Wooly Alder: August 13-18
Araneus orbweaver spider: August 19-24
Arbutus, Trailing: May 19-24
"army worms": June 13-18
Ash, Black: September 19-24, October 1-6
Ash, Mountain: January 19-24, October 7-12, December 1-6
ash seeds: January 7-12
Asian Ladybird Beetle: October 7-12
Aspen, Big-toothed: May 19-24, September 19-24
Aspen, Quaking: April 19-24, May 1-6, October 1-6, 7-12, December 7-12
Aster, Large-leaved: July 19-24, October 1-6
aurora borealis: November 13-18, December 25-31
Azure, Spring: May 1-6

b

backswimmers: January 1-6
Bald Eagle: March 25-31, November 7-12
Bald-faced Hornet: July 25-31, September 13-18
balm of Gilead: May 13-18, June 7-12
Balsam Fir: February 7-12
Balsam Poplar: May 13-18, June 7-12
Baltimore Oriole: May 13-18
Baneberry, Red: August 25-31
Baneberry, White: August 25-31
bark beetles: January 25-31
Barred Owl: January 25-31, March 1-6
Baskettail, Spiny: June 1-6

Basswood, American April 25-30, September 19-24, October 1-6, November 19-24
Bat, Little Brown: July 19-24
bats: December 1-6
Beach Pea: June 25-30
Beaked Hazel: April 13-18, July 1-6
Bear, Black: April 1-6, June 1-6, July 13-18, September 7-12, December 1-6
Beaver: January 19-24, October 25-31
Beetle, Asian Ladybird: October 7-12
Beetle, Divergent Metallic Wood-Borer: September 13-18
Beetle, Goldenrod Soldier: August 25-31
Beetle, Pine Sawyer: July 7-12
beetle, predaceous diving: January 1-6
beetles, bark: January 25-31
beetles, tiger: September 1-6
Big-toothed Aspen: May 19-24, September 19-24
Bindweed, Fringed: July 19-24
birch buds: January 7-12
Birch Conk: December 13-18
Birch, Paper: March 19-24, October 1-6, December 7-12
birch seeds: December 7-12
Bittern, American: May 1-6
Black Ash: September 19-24, October 1-6
Black Bear: April 1-6, June 1-6, July 13-18, September 7-12, December 1-6
Black-capped Chickadee: January 7-12, December 7-12
Black Spruce: February 7-12, July 19-24
Black-tipped Darner: September 1-6
Blackbird, Red-winged: March 13-18, April 1-6
"Blue" Goose: October 19-24
Blue Jay: August 13-18, September 13-18
Blue Stain: October 25-31
Bluebead Lily: June 7-12
blueberries: July 13-18, August 1-6
Bluebird, Eastern: April 1-6, September 7-12
Bobcat: February 13-18
Bobolink: May 25-31
Bohemian Waxwing: December 1-6
Boletus fungus: July 13-18
Bonaparte's Gull: May 13-18
Boreal Chorus Frog: April 19-24
Boreal Owl: February 7-12
Bosque del Apache National Wildlife Refuge: October 13-18, 19-24
Box Elder: March 19-24
Bracken Fern: August 7-12
Broad-winged Hawk: September 13-18
Brown-eyed Susan: July 25-31
bumblebees: May 1-6

Bunchberry: June 7-12, August 1-6, October 13-18
Bunting, Snow: October 19-24, November 13-18
butterflies: March 25-31, May 1-6, December 1-6
Butterfly, Monarch: August 19-24
Butterfly, Harvester: August 13-18
Butterfly, Spring Azure: May 1-6

c

calcium: January 25-31
Canada Darner: September 1-6
Canada Mayflower: June 7-12
"Canadian carpet": June 7-12
Canadian Tiger Swallowtail: June 1-6
"candle ice": April 13-18
Carpenter Ant: February 25-29
Caterpillar, Eastern Forest Tent: June 13-18
Caterpillar, Wooly Bear: September 25-30, December 1-6
catbirds: October 7-12
catkins: April 19-24
cattails: October 25-31
Cecropia Moth: July 7-12
Cedar, Northern White: November 19-24
Cedar Waxwing: August 7-12
"chandelier ice": April 13-18
Chanterelle: August 1-6
Chickadee, Black-capped: January 7-12, December 7-12
Chipmunk, Eastern: March 19-24, December 1-6
Chipmunk, Least: December 1-6
chipmunks: July 7-12
Chokecherry: May 25-31, October 1-6
Cirrus clouds: January 1-6
Cliff Swallow: May 13-18
Clintonia: June 7-12
clouds, cirrus: January 1-6
club moss: November 1-6
Columbine, Wild: May 25-31
Comma, Eastern: March 25-31
Common Goldeneye: February 1-6
Common Grackle: April 1-6, August 1-6
Common Green Darner: April 25-30, September 7-12
Common Loon: April 13-18, September 25-30
Common Merganser: February 1-6
Common Milkweed: November 19-24
Common Nighthawk: May 25-31, August 25-31
Common Raven: January 13-18, March 7-12
Common Redpoll: December 7-12
communal breeding: March 25-31
Comptons Tortoiseshell: March 25-31
Conifer False Morel: May 13-18

onk, Birch: December 13-18
otton-grass: July 19-24
ottontail, Eastern: February 7-12
ottonwood: June 7-12
oyote: January 13-18
ranberry, Highbush: October 7-12
ranberry, Mountain: June 25-30
rane, Sandhill: October 13-18
row, American: March 25-31

d

aisy, Ox-eye: July 25-31
amselflies: June 25-30
ark-eyed Junco: April 1-6, October 13-18
ark Fishing Spider: August 7-12
arner, Black-tipped: September 1-6
arner, Canada: September 1-6
arner, Common Green: April 25-30,
    September 1-6, 7-12
arner, Lake: September 1-6
arner, Zigzag: September 1-6
eer Mouse: January 25-31
eer, White-tailed: February 7-12, March 1-6,
    June 1-6, September 1-6,
    November 7-12, 19-24
iamond Willow: March 19-24
ivergent Metallic Wood-Borer Beetle:
    September 13-18
ogbane, Spreading: July 19-24, August 13-18
ogwood berries: September 7-12
ogwood, Red Osier: February 19-24,
    June 19-24, November 19-24
doll's-eyes": August 25-31
ove, Mourning: April 1-6
owitchers: August 1-6
owny Woodpecker: December 7-12
ragonflies: April 25-30, June 1-6, 25-30,
    August 19-24, September 1-6
ragonfly nymphs: January 1-6
rumming: April 19-24
uck, Long-tailed: October 25-31
ucks: April 7-12
uluth: March 25-31

e

agle, Bald: March 25-31, November 7-12
astern Bluebird: April 1-6, September 7-12
astern Chipmunk: March 19-24, December 1-6
astern Comma: March 25-31
astern Cottontail: February 7-12
astern Forest Tent Caterpillar: June 13-18
astern Garter Snake: April 7-12, December 1-6
astern Gray Tree Frog: May 7-12

Eastern Phoebe: April 13-18, August 7-12
Ebony Jewelwing: June 25-30
Elderberry, Red: May 19-24
"ermine": November 13-18
European Skipper: June 25-30
European Starling: March 7-12, October 1-6
Evening Grosbeak: January 7-12
Eyelash Cup: October 25-31

f

fawns: June 1-6
Fern, Bracken: August 7-12
Fern, Interrupted: June 1-6
finches: January 7-12
Fir, Balsam: February 7-12, October 25-31
fire: July 19-24
firefly: June 13-18
Fireweed: July 19-24, August 7-12,
    September 19-24
Fisher: February 13-18
Flicker, Northern: September 19-24
Fly Amanita: August 13-18
Fly, Gall: January 25-31
Fly, Sarcophagus: June 13-18
Fly Honeysuckle, Northern: July 1-6
Flying Squirrel, Northern: February 13-18, 19-24,
    March 1-6, December 13-18
Fox Sparrow: October 13-18
Franklin's Ground Squirrel: September 7-12,
    December 1-6
Franklin's Gull: March 13-18
Fringed Bindweed: July 19-24
Fringed Polygala: June 1-6
Frog, Boreal Chorus: April 19-24
Frog, Eastern Gray Tree: May 7-12
Frog, Green: June 19-24
Frog, Leopard: May 7-12
Frog, Mink: June 7-12
Frog, Wood: April 19-24, September 19-24
Froghopper: June 19-24
frogs: December 1-6
frost: September 1-6
Fungus, Blue Stain: October 25-31
Fungus, Scarlet Cup: April 25-30

g

Gall Fly: January 25-31
gall, goldenrod: January 25-31
gall, willow-cone: November 25-30
Garter Snake, Eastern: April 7-12, December 1-6
giant water bug: January 1-6
Gilbert, Jim: August 19-24
glycerol: September 19-24

Goldeneye, Common: February 1-6
Goldenrod Crab Spider: July 25-31
goldenrod gall: Januray 25-31
Goldenrod Soldier Beetle: August 25-31
Goldenrod, Zigzag: August 25-31
goldenrods: July 25-31, August 25-31
Goldfinch, American: August 7-12, December 1-6
Goose, "Blue": October 19-24
Goose, Snow: October 19-24
gooseberries: August 1-6
Goshawk, Northern: October 13-18
Grackle, Common: April 1-6, August 1-6
Grand Marais, Minnesota: October 25-31
grasshoppers: August 19-24
Gray Jay: January 13-18
Gray Squirrel: February 13-18, September 25-30
Great Gray Owl: December 19-24
Great Horned Owl: February 19-24
Green Frog: June 19-24
green up: May 1-6
Green-winged Teal: April 7-12
Grosbeak, Evening: January 7-12
Grosbeak, Pine: January 7-12
Ground Squirrel, Franklin's: September 7-12,
    December 1-6
grouse: August 1-6
Grouse, Ruffed: February 1-6, April 19-24,
    October 13-18, December 7-12
Grouse, Sharp-tailed: April 19-24
Gull, Bonaparte's: May 13-18
Gull, Franklin's: March 13-18
Gull, Herring: March 13-18
Gull, Ring-billed: March 13-18

h

Hare, Snowshoe: February 7-12, October 13-18,
    November 13-18
hares: March 13-18
Harris's Sparrow: October 13-18
Harvester Butterfly: August 13-18
Hawk, Broad-winged: September 13-18
Hawk, Rough-legged: November 7-12
Hawk Ridge: September 7-12, 13-18,
    October 1-6, 13-18
Hazel, Beaked: April 13-18, July 1-6
Hepatica, Round-lobed: April 13-18
Herring Gull: March 13-18
Highbush Cranberry: October 7-12
hoar frost: November 19-24
honeydew: July 25-31
Honeysuckle, Northern Fly: July 1-6
Hornet, Bald-faced: July 25-31, September 13-18
Hummingbird, Ruby-throated: May 25-31

i

ice: January 13-18, December 19-24
ice-out: April 13-18, October 25-31
ice types: April 13-18
ice up: November 7-12, 25-30
Indian-Pipe: July 13-18
Interrupted Fern: June 1-6
Inuit: July 19-24
irruptive species: January 7-12
Isabella Moth: September 25-30

j

Jaeger, Parasitic: September 13-18
January thaw: January 7-12
Jay, Blue: August 13-18, September 13-18
Jay, Gray: January 13-18
Jewelwing, Ebony: June 25-30
Junco, Dark-eyed: April 1-6
Juneberry: May 25-31, August 1-6

k

Kestrel, American: September 7-12
Kinglet, Ruby-crowned: May 1-6

l

Ladybird Beetle: October 7-12
Ladyslipper, Pink: June 7-12, July 1-6
Ladyslipper, Showy: July 1-6
Ladyslipper, Yellow: July 1-6
Lake Darner: September 1-6
Lake Superior: September 13-18, October 25-31, November 7-12
Lake Superior agate: November 7-12
Large-flowered Trillium: May 13-18
Large-leaved Aster: July 19-24, October 1-6
Least Chipmunk: December 1-6
Least Weasel: November 13-18
Leeks, Wild: June 7-12
lek: April 19-24
Leopard Frog: May 7-12
Lightning Bug: June 13-18
Lincoln's Sparrow: October 13-18
Linden Looper: October 25-31
Lingonberry: June 25-30
Little Brown Bat: July 19-24
long-jawed orbweaver spider: August 25-31
Long-tailed Duck: October 25-31
Long-tailed Weasel: November 13-18
Loon, Common: April 13-18, September 25-30
Luna Moth: June 7-12
Lupine, Wild: July 7-12
Lycopodium: November 1-6

m

Magnolia Warbler: May 19-24
Mallard: February 1-6
maple buds: January 7-12
Maple, Moose: July 1-6
Maple, Mountain: July 1-6
Maple, Red: March 19-24, May 1-6
maple seeds: September 25-30
Maple, Sugar: February 13-18, March 19-24,
    May 1-6, August 25-31, October 1-6,
    November 19-24
mare's tails: January 1-6
Marigold, Marsh: May 1-6
Marsh Marigold: May 1-6
Marten, Pine: December 7-12
Mayflower, Canada: June 7-12
meadowhawk: August 19-24
Merganser, Common: February 1-6
methyl hydrazine: May 13-18
Mexico: August 19-24, September 7-12
mice: March 13-18
Milbert's Tortoiseshell: March 25-31
Milkweed, Common: November 19-24
Mink Frog: June 7-12
Mississippi River: March 25-31, November 7-12
Moccasin Flower: July 1-6
mold, slime: July 13-18
Monarch: August 19-24
Moose: January 25-31, November 25-30,
    December 19-24, 25-31
Moose Maple: July 1-6
Morel, Conifer False: May 13-18
mosquitoes: April 25-30
Moth, Cecropia: July 7-12
Moth, Isabella: September 25-30
Moth, Luna: June 7-12
Moth, Polyphemus: July 7-12
Moth, White-lined Sphinx: August 13-18
Mountain Ash: January 19-24, October 7-12,
    December 1-6
Mountain Cranberry: June 25-30
Mountain Maple: July 1-6
Mourning Cloak: March 25-31
Mourning Dove: April 1-6
Mouse, Deer: January 25-31
Mouse, White-footed: January 25-31
Mushroom, Oyster: July 7-12
Mushroom, Shaggy Mane: October 25-31
Muskrat: October 25-31

n

Nebraska: October 13-18

New Mexico: October 13-18
Nighthawk, Common: May 25-31, August 25-31
North Shore: October 1-6
Northern Flicker: September 19-24
Northern Fly Honeysuckle: July 1-6
Northern Flying Squirrel: February 13-18, 19-24,
    March 1-6, December 13-18
Northern Goshawk: October 13-18
Northern Hawk-Owl: December 19-24
northern lights: November 13-18,
    December 25-31
Northern Red Oak: December 25-31
Northern Shrike: March 1-6
Northern White Cedar: November 19-24
nuptial plumage: April 7-12
Nuthatch, Red-breasted: December 7-12
Nuthatch, White-breasted: December 7-12

o

Oak, Northern Red: October 1-6,
    December 25-31
Oak, White: December 25-31
oaks: April 25-30,: September 7-12
Ojibwa Indians: August 25-31
oldsquaw: October 25-31
orbweaver spiders: August 19-24, 25-31
Oriole, Baltimore: May 13-18
Otter, River: February 13-18
Ovenbird: May 7-12
Owl, Barred: January 25-31, March 1-6
Owl, Boreal: February 7-12
Owl, Great Gray: December 19-24
Owl, Great Horned: February 19-24
Owl, Northern Hawk-: December 19-24
Owl, Saw-whet: February 25-29, March 1-6,
    October 1-6
Ox-eye Daisy: July 25-31
Oyster Mushroom: July 7-12

p

Painted Turtle, Western: April 25-30, June 19-24,
    December 1-6
Palm Warbler: September 25-30
Paper Birch: March 19-24
Paper Wasp: September 13-18
Parasitic Jaeger: September 13-18
parhelia: January 19-24
Pea, Beach: June 25-30
Pheobe, Eastern: April 13-18, August 7-12
Pileated Woodpecker: February 25-29
piloerection: January 7-12
Pin Cherry: May 25-31, July 7-12, August 1-6
Pine Marten: December 7-12

ine Sawyer Beetle: July 7-12
ine, White: February 13-18, June 19-24
ines: October 25-31
ink Ladyslipper: June 7-12, July 1-6
itcher Plant: June 13-18
lantain leaves: September 25-30
latte River: October 13-18
lum, Wild: May 25-31
ollen: June 19-24
olygala, Fringed: June 1-6
olyphemus Moth: July 7-12
opal: April 19-24, May 1-6, October 1-6, 7-12,
    December 7-12
oplar, Balsam: May 13-18, June 7-12
orcupine: February 13-18, March 19-24
redaceous diving beetle: January 1-6
ussy Willow: March 19-24

Quaking Aspen: April 19-24, May 1-6,
    October 1-6, 7-12, December 7-12

abbits: March 13-18
Raccoon: March 1-6, November 25-30
Rail, Virginia: August 25-31
aspberries: August 1-6
Raven, Common: January 13-18, March 7-12
Red-backed Vole: March 1-6
Red Baneberry: August 25-31
Red-bellied Snake: May 19-24, December 1-6
Red-berried Elder: May 19-24
Red-breasted Nuthatch: December 7-12
Red Elderberry: May 19-24
Red-eyed Vireo: August 19-24
Red Fox: March 7-12
Red Maple: March 19-24, May 1-6
Red Oak, Northern: October 1-6,
    December 25-31
Red Osier Dogwood: February 19-24,
    June 19-24, November 19-24
Red Squirrel: January 19-24, 25-31, February 1-6,
    March 1-6, 7-12, July 1-6, 25-31
Red-winged Blackbird: March 13-18, April 1-6
Redpoll, Common: December 7-12
Rice, Wild: August 25-31
rice birds": August 25-31
Ring-billed Gull: March 13-18
River Otter: February 13-18
Robin, American: March 25-31, August 7-12,
    October 1-6, 7-12, 19-24
odents: January 25-31
Rose family: May 25-31

Rough-legged Hawk: November 7-12
Round-lobed Hepatica: April 13-18
Ruby-crowned Kinglet: May 1-6
Ruby-throated Hummingbird: May 25-31
Ruffed Grouse: February 1-6, April 19-24,
    October 13-18, December 7-12

S

salamanders: December 1-6
samara: September 25-30
Sandhill Crane: October 13-18
sandpipers: August 1-6
sap: March 25-31
sap, birch: March 7-12
sap, maple: March 7-12
Sapsucker, Yellow-bellied: March 7-12, April 25-30
Sarcophagus Flies: June 13-18
Savannah Sparrow: October 13-18
Saw-whet Owl: February 25-29, March 1-6,
    October 1-6
Scandinavia: July 19-24, December 7-12
Scarlet Cup Fungi: April 25-30
"seagull": March 13-18
sedges: July 19-24
seeds: January 19-24
seeds, ash: January 7-12
Shaggy Mane Mushroom: October 25-31
Sharp-tailed Grouse: April 19-24
shorebirds: August 1-6
Short-tailed Weasel: November 13-18
Showy Ladyslipper: July 1-6
Shrike, Northern: March 1-6
Siberia: July 19-24, December 7-12
Skimmer, Twelve-spotted: June 25-30
Skipper, European: June 25-30
Skunk Currant: August 1-6
Skunk, Striped: February 25-29
slime molds: July 13-18
Snake, Eastern Garter: April 7-12, December 1-6
Snake, Red-bellied: May 19-24, December 1-6
Snapping Turtle: December 1-6
snow: January 13-18, February 7-12,
    March 7-12, October 19-24
Snow Bunting: October 19-24, November 13-18
Snow Flea: December 25-31
Snow Goose: October 19-24
Snowshoe Hare: February 7-12, October 13-18,
    November 13-18
Snowy Owl: January 1-6
Solitaire, Townsend's: January 19-24
Song Sparrow: October 13-18
Sparrow, American Tree: October 13-18
Sparrow, Fox: October 13-18

Sparrow, Harris's: October 13-18
Sparrow, Lincoln's: October 13-18
Sparrow, Savannah: October 13-18
Sparrow, White-crowned: October 13-18
Sparrow, White-throated: October 13-18
sparrows: September 1-6
Speckled Alder: April 19-24, August 13-18
spider, Araneus orbweaver: August 19-24
Spider, Dark Fishing: August 7-12
Spider, Goldenrod Crab: July 25-31
spider, long-jawed orbweaver: August 25-31
Spider, Wolf: July 1-6
spiders: March 1-6, October 1-6
Spiny Baskettail: June 1-6
Spittlebug: June 19-24
Spreading Dogbane: July 19-24, August 13-18
Spring Azure Butterfly: May 1-6
Spring Peeper: April 19-24
Springtail: December 25-31
Spruce, Black: February 7-12, July 19-24
spruce cones: July 25-31
Spruce, White: February 7-12, 13-18
spruces: May 19-24, July 13-18, October 25-31
Squirrel, Franklin's Ground: September 7-12,
    December 1-6
Squirrel, Gray: February 13-18, September 25-30
Squirrel, Northern Flying: February 13-18, 19-24,
    March 1-6, December 13-18
Squirrel, Red: January 19-24, 25-31, February 1-6,
    March 1-6, 7-12, July 1-6, 25-31
St. Louis River: April 1-6
Staghorn Sumac: September 7-12, October 1-6
Starflower: June 7-12
Starling, European: March 7-12, October 1-6
stars: September 1-6
Striped Skunk: February 25-29
Sugar Maple: February 13-18, March 19-24,
    May 1-6, August 25-31, October 1-6,
    November 19-24
Sumac, Staghorn: September 7-12, October 1-6
sundogs: January 19-24
Swallow, Cliff: May 13-18
Swallow, Tree: April 1-6, 19-24
Swallowtail, Canadian Tiger: June 1-6
Swan, Tundra: April 1-6

t

Tamarack: May 7-12, October 19-24
Texas: September 13-18
Thimbleberry: July 25-31
thrashers: October 7-12
Thrush, Varied: January 19-24
thrushes: September 1-6, October 7-12

"thunder snow": December 1-6
Tick, Wood: May 7-12
tiger beetles: September 1-6
Timber Wolf: February 25-29
tinder polypore: December 13-18
Toad, American: May 25-31
Tortoiseshell, Comptons: March 25-31
Tortoiseshell, Milbert's: March 25-31
Townsend's Solitaire: January 19-24
Trailing Arbutus: May 19-24
Tree Swallow: April 1-6, 19-24
Trillium, Large-flowered: May 13-18
Tundra Swan: April 1-6
Turtle, Snapping: December 1-6
Turtle, Western Painted: April 25-30,
    June 19-24, December 1-6
Twelve-spotted Skimmer: June 25-30
Twinflower: June 7-12

U

Urquhart, Dr. Fred: August 19-24

V

Varied Thrush: January 19-24
velvet: September 1-6
Vikings: August 13-18
Vireo, Red-eyed: August 19-24
Virginia Creeper: September 7-12, 19-24
Virginia Rail: August 25-31
Vole, Red-backed: March 1-6
voles: January 13-18
voyageurs: December 13-18

W

Warbler, Magnolia: May 19-24
Warbler, Palm: September 25-30
Warbler, Yellow-rumped: September 25-30
warblers: May 7-12,: August 13-18,
    September 1-6
Wasp, Paper: September 13-18
water boatmen: January 1-6
Waxwing, Bohemian: December 1-6
Waxwing, Cedar: August 7-12
waxwings: October 7-12
Weasel, Least: November 13-18
Weasel, Long-tailed: November 13-18
Weasel, Short-tailed: November 13-18
webs, spider: August 19-24
Western Painted Turtle: April 25-30, June 19-24,
    December 1-6
Whip-poor-will: June 1-6
"whiskey jack": January 13-18
White Baneberry: August 25-31

White-breasted Nuthatch: December 7-12
White-crowned Sparrow: October 13-18
White-footed Mouse: January 25-31
White Oak: December 25-31
White Pine: February 13-18, June 19-24
White Spruce: February 7-12, 13-18
White-tailed Deer: February 7-12, March 1-6,
    June 1-6, September 1-6, November 7-12,
    November 19-24, December 25-31
White-throated Sparrow: October 13-18
Wild Columbine: May 25-31
Wild Leeks: June 7-12
Wild Lupine: July 7-12
Wild Plum: May 25-31
Wild Rice: August 25-31
Willow, Diamond: March 19-24
Willow, Pussy: March 19-24
willow-cone gall: November 25-30
willows: February 7-12, 19-24, November 19-24
windchills: January 1-6
Winter Wren: May 1-6
Wintergreen: October 25-31
wolf spiders: July 1-6, August 7-12
Wolf, Timber: January 13-18, February 25-29
wolves: January 13-18
Wood Frog: April 19-24, September 19-24
Wood Tick: May 7-12
Woodchuck: April 1-6, December 1-6
Woodcock, American: April 7-12
Woodpecker, Downy: December 7-12
Woodpecker, Pileated: February 25-29
woodpeckers: April 25-30, July 1-6,
    September 19-24
Wooly Alder Aphid: August 13-18
Wooly Bear Caterpillar: September 25-30,
    December 1-6
Wren, Winter: May 1-6

Y

Yellow-bellied Sapsucker: March 7-12, April 25-30
Yellow Ladyslipper: July 1-6
Yellow-rumped Warbler: September 25-30
yellowlegs: August 1-6

Z

Zigzag Darner: September 1-6
Zigzag Goldenrod: August 25-31